Ancient Texts and the Bible
Book 1 - Easy Reader Edition

In The Beginning...
From Adam to Noah

Minister 2 Others

Ancient Texts and the Bible
Book 1

In The Beginning...
From Adam to Noah

Easy Reader Edition

In The Beginning... From Adam to Noah
ISBN 978-1-947751-18-7

Ancient texts compiled for this series:

The Bible
King James Version 1769

The Book of Enoch
An English translation by Dr. Laurence,
Archbishop of Cashel,
Formerly professor of Hebrew at Oxford, 1833

The Book of Jasher
Faithfully translated 1840
From the original Hebrew into English
Published by J.H. Parry & Company 1887

The Book of Jubilees
By R.H. Charles, Oxford: Clarendon Press, 1913

Ancient Texts and the Bible

series include:

Book 1: In The Beginning... From Adam to Noah

Book 2: In The Beginning... From Noah to Abraham

Book 3: In The Beginning... From Abraham to Israel

Book 4: In The Beginning... From Israel to Egypt

Book 5: In The Beginning... From Egypt to Goshen

Book 6: Israel... From Goshen to Sinai

Book 7: Israel... From Sinai to the Tabernacle

Book 8: Israel... Through the Book of Leviticus

Book 9: Israel... Through the Book of Numbers

Book 10: Israel... Through the Book of Joshua

Table of Contents:

Forward

The **Ancient Texts and the Bible** series synchronizes the manuscripts of Enoch, Jasher, and Jubilees into the Bible, making one complete storyline. The books are interwoven using the Torah as the backbone, and the extra-biblical texts as the fleshing out of that backbone.

The first book in the series contains Genesis chapters 1 - 5, as well as parts in the following books: Enoch chapters 3 - 5, 22 - 35, 37 - 43, 45 - 52, 58 - 62, 68 - 90, 92 - 105; Jasher chapters 1 - 4; and Jubilees chapters 2 - 4, and 50.

Though the language in the writings have been updated, replacing words like "*thou*" and "*thine*" with words like "*you*" and "*your*", the integrity of the verses remain.

The "*Easy Reader*" edition is for those who just want to read the storyline and enjoy the journey. The stop signs and complex formatting have been removed so one may merely focus upon the story being told.

The *Expanded Edition* of **Ancient Texts and the Bible** was created for the more studious reader. The various manuscripts have the following formatting applied to them in this edition:

the Bible - Regular

THE BOOK OF ENOCH - ALL CAPITALS

the Book of Jasher - Italics

<u>the Book of Jubilees - Underlined</u>

Where one of the extra-biblical texts reiterates the Bible, the phrase is then put in a **bold font**. Where two manuscripts overlap each other exclusive of the Bible, then both fonts are used. For instance, where Jasher and Jubilees intercept, the text is then formatted as *Italics and Underlined.*

The stop sign is another element to the *Expanded Edition* that is not seen in the *Easy Reader*. This image points to contradictions in the content. Printed versions also contain page numbers within the stop sign revealing the page where contradictory information is located, and vice versa. This information was not feasible to place in the e-book versions since the page numbers vary depending on the font size the reader chooses. Following, is an example from each edition:

Easy Reader Edition:

(Genesis 1:27) (...Jasher 1:1) (Jubilees 2:14...)
And after all this God created man in His own image, He created him in the image of God; He created them male and female, a man and a woman.

Expanded Edition:

(Genesis 1:27) (...Jasher 1:1) (Jubilees 2:14...)
And after all this **God created man *in His own image,*** He created him in the image of God; **He created them** male and female, a man and a woman.

Whichever you choose, may you ***Enjoy the Journey***!

Prologue

(Jubilees 2:1)
And the angel of the presence spoke to Moses according to the word of the Lord, saying: Write the complete history of the creation, how in six days the Lord God finished all His works and all that He created, and kept Sabbath on the seventh day and hallowed it for all ages, and appointed it as a sign for all His works.

(Jubilees Intro)
THIS is the history of the division of the days of the law and of the testimony, of the events of the years, of their weeks, of their Jubilees throughout all the years of the world, as the Lord spoke to Moses on Mount Sinai when he went up to receive the tables of the law and of the commandment, according to the voice of God as he said to him, Go up to the top of the Mount.

Genesis: Chapter One

(Genesis 1:1)
In the beginning God created the heaven and the earth.

(Genesis 1:2)
And the earth was without form, and void; and darkness was on the face of the deep. And the Spirit of God moved on the face of the waters.

(Genesis 1:3)
And God said, Let there be light: and there was light.

(Genesis 1:4)
And God saw the light, that it was good: and God divided the light from the darkness.

(Genesis 1:5)
And God called the light Day, and the darkness He called Night. And the evening and the morning were the first day.

(Jubilees 2:2)
For on the first day He created the heavens which are above and the earth and the waters and all the spirits which serve before Him - the angels of the presence, and the angels of sanctification, and the angels of the spirit of fire and the angels of the spirit of the winds, and the angels of the spirit of the clouds, and of darkness, and of snow and of hail and of hoar frost, and the angels of the voices and of the thunder and of the lightning, and the angels of the spirits of cold and of heat, and of winter and of spring and of autumn and of summer

and of all the spirits of His creatures which are in the heavens and on the earth, He created the abysses and the darkness, eventide and night, and the light, dawn and day, which He has prepared in the knowledge of His heart.

(Jubilees 2:3)
And thereupon we saw His works, and praised Him, and lauded before Him on account of all His works; for seven great works He created on the first day.

(Genesis 1:6)

And God said, Let there be a firmament in the midst of the waters, and let it divide the waters from the waters.

(Genesis 1:7) (Jubilees 2:4)

And on the second day God made the firmament, in the midst of the waters and divided the waters on that day which were under the firmament from the waters which were above the firmament: half of them went up above and half of them went down below the firmament that was in the midst over the face of the whole earth. And this was the only work God created on the second day, and it was so.

(Genesis 1:8)

And God called the firmament Heaven. And the evening and the morning were the second day.

(Genesis 1:9) (Jubilees 2:5)

And on the third day God said, Let the waters under the heaven be gathered together, to pass from off the face of the whole earth to one place, and let the dry land appear: and it was so.

(Jubilees 2:6)
And the waters did as He commanded them, and they retired from off the face of the earth into one place outside of this firmament, and the dry land appeared.

(Jubilees 2:7)
And on that day, He created for them all the seas according to their separate gathering-places, and all the rivers, and the gatherings of the waters in the mountains and on all the earth, and all the lakes, and all the dew of the earth.

(Genesis 1:10)
And God called the dry land Earth; and the gathering together of the waters He called Seas: and God saw that it was good.

~ ~ ~

(Enoch 75:1)
And at the extremities of the earth I beheld twelve gates open for all the winds, from which they proceed and blow over the earth.

(Enoch 75:2)
Three of them are open in the front of heaven, three in the west, three on the right side of heaven, and three on the left. The first three are those which are towards the east, three are towards the north, three behind those which are on the left, towards the south, and three on the west.

(Enoch 75:3)
From four of them proceed winds of blessing, and of health; and from eight proceed winds of punishment; when they

are sent to destroy the earth, and the heaven above it, all its inhabitants, and all which are in the waters, or on dry land.

(Enoch 75:4)
The first of these winds proceeds from the gate termed the eastern, through the first gate on the east, which inclines southwards. From this goes forth destruction, drought, heat, and perdition.

(Enoch 75:5)
From the second gate, the middle one, proceeds equity. There issue from it rain, fruitfulness, health, and dew; and from the third gate northwards, proceed cold and drought.

(Enoch 75:6)
After these proceed the south winds through three principal gates; through their first gate, which inclines eastwards, proceeds a hot wind.

(Enoch 75:7)
But from the middle gate proceed grateful odor, dew, rain, health, and life.

(Enoch 75:8)
From the third gate, which is westwards, proceed dew, rain, blight, and destruction.

(Enoch 75:9)
After these are the winds to the north, which is called the sea. They proceed from three gates. The first gate is that which is on the east, inclining southwards; from this proceed dew, rain, blight, and destruction. From the middle direct gate proceed rain, dew, life, and health. And from the third gate, which is

westwards, inclining towards the south, proceed mist, frost, snow, rain, dew, and blight.

(Enoch 75:10)
After these in the fourth quarter are the winds to the west. From the first gate, inclining northwards, proceed dew, rain, frost, cold, snow, and chill; from the middle gate proceed rain, health, and blessing;

(Enoch 75:11)
And from the last gate, which is southwards, proceed drought, destruction, scorching, and perdition.

(Enoch 75:12)
The account of the twelve gates of the four quarters of heaven is ended.

(Enoch 75:13)
All their laws, all their infliction of punishment, and the health produced by them, have I explained to you, my son Mathusala.

~ ~ ~

(Enoch 76:1)
The first wind is called the eastern, because it is the first.

(Enoch 76:2)
The second is called the south, because the Most High there descends, and frequently there descends he who is blessed forever.

(Enoch 76:3)
The western wind has the name of diminution, because there all the luminaries of heaven are diminished, and descend.

(Enoch 76:4)
The fourth wind, which is named the north, is divided into three parts; one of which is for the habitation of man; another for seas of water, with valleys, woods, rivers, shady places, and snow; and the third part contains paradise.

(Enoch 76:5)
Seven high mountains I beheld, higher than all the mountains of the earth, from which frost proceeds; while days, seasons, and years depart and pass away.

(Enoch 76:6)
Seven rivers I beheld on earth, greater than all rivers, one of which takes its course from the west; into a great sea its water flows.

(Enoch 76:7)
Two come from the north to the sea, their waters flowing into the Erythræan Sea, on the east. And with respect to the remaining four, they take their course in the cavity of the north, two to their sea, the Erythræan Sea, and two are poured into a great sea, where also it is said there is a desert.

(Enoch 76:8)
Seven great islands I saw in the sea and on the earth. Seven in the great sea.

(Genesis 1:11)

And God said, Let the earth bring forth grass, the herb yielding seed, and the fruit tree yielding fruit after his kind, whose seed is in itself, on the earth: and it was so.

(Genesis 1:12) (Jubilees 2:7)
And the earth brought forth grass, and herb yielding seed after his kind, and the seed which is sown, and all sprouting things and the fruit tree, whose seed was in itself, after his kind: and trees of the wood, and the Garden of Eden, in Eden and all plants after their kind. And God saw that it was good.

(Jubilees 2:8...)
These four great works God created on the third day.

~ ~ ~

(Enoch 25:1)
From there I proceeded to the middle of the earth, and beheld a happy and fertile spot, which contained branches continually sprouting from the trees which were planted in it. There I saw a holy mountain, and underneath it water on the eastern side, which flowed towards the south. I saw also on the east another mountain as high as that; and between them there were deep, but not wide valleys.

(Enoch 25:2)
Water ran towards the mountain to the west of this; and underneath there was likewise another mountain.

(Enoch 25:3)
There was a valley, but not a wide one, below it; and in the midst of them were other deep and dry valleys towards the extremity of the three. All these valleys, which were deep,

but not wide, consisted of a strong rock, with a tree which was planted in them. And I wondered at the rock and at the valleys, being extremely surprised.

~ ~ ~

(Enoch 26:1)
Then I said, What does this blessed land mean, all these lofty trees, and the accursed valley between them?

(Enoch 26:2)
Then Uriel, one of the holy angels who were with me, replied, This valley is the accursed of the accursed forever. Here shall be collected all who utter with their mouths unbecoming language against God, and speak harsh things of his glory. Here shall they be collected. Here shall be their territory.

(Enoch 26:3)
In the latter days, an example of judgment shall be made of them in righteousness before the saints: while those who have received mercy shall forever, all their days, bless God, the Everlasting King.

(Enoch 26:4)
And at the period of judgment shall they bless him for his mercy, as he has distributed it to them. Then I blessed God, addressing myself to him, and making mention, as was meet, of his greatness.

~ ~ ~

(Enoch 27:1)
From there I proceeded towards the east, to the middle of the mountain in the desert, the level surface only of which I perceived.

(Enoch 27:2)
It was full of trees of the seed alluded to; and water leaped down on it.

(Enoch 27:3)
There appeared a cataract composed as of many cataracts both towards the west and towards the east. On one side were trees; on the other water and dew.

~ ~ ~

(Enoch 28:1)
Then I went to another place from the desert, towards the east of that mountain which I had approached.

(Enoch 28:2)
There I beheld choice trees, particularly those which produce the sweet-smelling drugs, frankincense and myrrh; and trees unlike to each other.

(Enoch 28:3)
And over it, above them, was the elevation of the eastern mountain at no great distance.

~ ~ ~

(Enoch 29:1)
I likewise saw another place with valleys of water which never wasted,

(Enoch 29:2)
Where I perceived a goodly tree, which in smell resembled zasakinon.

(Enoch 29:3)
And towards the sides of these valleys I perceived cinnamon of a sweet odor. Over them I advanced towards the east.

~ ~ ~

(Enoch 30:1)
Then I beheld another mountain containing trees, from which water flowed like Neketro. Its name was Sarira, and Kalboneba. And on this mountain, I beheld another mountain, on which were trees of alva.

(Enoch 30:2)
These trees were full, like almond trees, and strong; and when they produced fruit, it was superior to all perfume.

(Genesis 1:13)

And the evening and the morning were the third day.

(Genesis 1:14)

And God said, Let there be lights in the firmament of the heaven to divide the day from the night; and let them be for signs, and for seasons, and for days, and years.

~ ~ ~

(Enoch 81: 5)
With respect to the progress of the sun in heaven, it enters and goes out of each gate for thirty days, with the leaders of the thousand classes of the stars; with four which are added, and appertain to the four quarters of the year, which conduct them, and accompany them at four periods.

(Enoch 81:6)
Respecting these, men greatly err, and do not compute them in the computation of every age; for they greatly err respecting them; nor do men know accurately that they are in the computation of the year. But indeed, these are marked down forever; one in the first gate, one in the third, one in the fourth, and one in the sixth:

(Enoch 81:7)
So that the year is completed in three hundred and sixty-four days.

(Enoch 81:8)
Truly has been stated, and accurately has been computed that which is marked down; for the luminaries, the months, the fixed periods, the years, and the days, Uriel has explained to me, and communicated to me; whom the Lord of all creation, on my account, commanded (according to the might of heaven, and the power which it possesses both by night and by day) to explain the laws of light to man, of the sun, moon, and stars, and of all the powers of heaven, which are turned with their respective orbs.

(Enoch 81:9)
This is the ordinance of the stars, which set in their places, in their seasons, in their periods, in their days, and in their months.

(Enoch 81:10)
These are the names of those who conduct them, who watch and enter in their seasons, according to their ordinance in their periods, in their months, in the times of their influence, and in their stations.

(Enoch 81:11)
Four conductors of them first enter, who separate the four quarters of the year. After these, twelve conductors of their classes, who separate the months and the year into three hundred and sixty-four days, with the leaders of a thousand, who distinguish between the days, as well as between the four additional ones; which, as conductors, divide the four quarters of the year.

(Enoch 81:12)
These leaders of a thousand are in the midst of the conductors, and the conductors are added each behind his station, and their conductors make the separation. These are the names of the conductors, who separate the four quarters of the year, who are appointed over them: Melkel, Helammelak,

(Enoch 81:13)
Meliyal, and Narel.

(Enoch 81:14)
And the names of those who conduct them are Adnarel, Jyasusal, and Jyelumeal.

(Enoch 81:15)
These are the three who follow after the conductors of the classes of stars; each following after the three conductors of the classes, which themselves follow after those conductors of the stations, who divide the four quarters of the year.

(Enoch 81:16)
In the first part of the year rises and rules Melkyas, who is named Tamani, and Zahay.

(Enoch 81:17)
All the days of his influence, during which he rules, are ninety-one days.

(Enoch 81:18)
And these are the signs of the days which are seen on earth. In the days of his influence there is perspiration, heat, and trouble. All the trees become fruitful; the leaf of every tree comes forth; the corn is reaped; the rose and every species of flowers blossoms in the field; and the trees of winter are dried up.

(Enoch 81:19)
These are the names of the conductors who are under them: Arkel, Zelsabel; and another additional conductor of a thousand is named Heloyalef, the days of whose influence have been completed. The other conductor next after them is Helemmelek, whose name they call the Splendid Zahay.

(Enoch 81:20)
All the days of his light are ninety-one days.

(Enoch 81:21)
These are the signs of the days on earth, heat and drought;

while the trees bring forth their fruits, warmed and concocted, and give their fruits to dry.

(Enoch 81:22)
The flocks follow and yean. All the fruits of the earth are collected, with everything in the fields, and the vines are trodden. This takes place during the time of his influence.

(Enoch 81:23)
These are their names and orders, and the names of the conductors who are under them, of those who are chiefs of a thousand: Gedaeyal, Keel, Heel.

(Enoch 81:24)
And the name of the additional leader of a thousand is Asphael.

(Enoch 81:25)
The days of his influence have been completed.

(Genesis 1:15)
And let them be for lights in the firmament of the heaven to give light on the earth: and it was so.

(Genesis 1:16)
And God made two great lights; the greater light to rule the day, and the lesser light to rule the night: He made the stars also.

(Genesis 1:17) (...Jubilees 2:8)
And on the fourth day He created the sun and the moon and the stars, And God set them in the firmament of the heaven to give light on the earth.

(Jubilees 2:9)
And God appointed the sun to be a great sign on the earth for days and for sabbaths and for months and for feasts and for years and for sabbaths of years and for jubilees and for all seasons of the years.

(Genesis 1:18) (Jubilees 2:8, 10)
And to rule over the day and over the night, and to divide the light from the darkness for prosperity, that all things may prosper which shoot and grow on the earth. And God saw that it was good.

(Genesis 1:19) (Jubilees 2:11...)
These three kinds He made, and the evening and the morning were the fourth day.

~ ~ ~

(Enoch 23:1)
From there I went to another place, towards the west, to the extremities of the earth.

(Enoch 23:2)
Where I beheld a fire blazing and running along without cessation, which intermitted its course neither by day nor by night; but continued always the same.

(Enoch 23:3)
I inquired, saying, What is this, which never ceases?

(Enoch 23:4)
Then Raguel, one of the holy angels who were with me, answered,

(Enoch 23:5)
And said, This blazing fire, which you behold running towards the west, is that of all the luminaries of heaven.

~ ~ ~

(Enoch 32:1)
From there I went on towards the extremities of the earth; where I saw large beasts different from each other, and birds various in their countenances and forms, as well as with notes of different sounds.

(Enoch 32:2)
To the east of these beasts I perceived the extremities of the earth, where heaven ceased. The gates of heaven stood open, and I beheld the celestial stars come forth. I numbered them as they proceeded out of the gate, and wrote them all down, as they came out one by one according to their number. I wrote down their names altogether, their times and their seasons, as the angel Uriel, who was with me, pointed them out to me.

(Enoch 32:3)
He showed them all to me, and wrote down an account of them.

(Enoch 32:4)
He also wrote down for me their names, their regulations, and their operations.

~ ~ ~

(Enoch 41:4)
I beheld also the receptacles of the moon, where the moons came, where they proceeded, their glorious return, and how one became more splendid than another. I marked their rich progress, their unchangeable progress, their disunited and undiminished progress; their observance of a mutual fidelity by a stable oath; their proceeding forth before the sun, and their adherence to the path allotted them, in obedience to the command of the Lord of spirits. Potent is his name forever and forever.

(Enoch 41:5)
After this I perceived, that the path both concealed and manifest of the moon, as well as the progress of its path, was there completed by day and by night; while each, one with another, looked towards the Lord of spirits, magnifying and praising without cessation, since praise to them is rest; for in the splendid sun there is a frequent conversion to blessing and to malediction.

(Enoch 41:6)
The course of the moon's path to the righteous is light, but to sinners it is darkness; in the name of the Lord of spirits, who created a division between light and darkness, and, separating the spirits of men, strengthened the spirits of the righteous in the name of his own righteousness.

(Enoch 41:7)
Nor does the angel prevent this, neither is he endowed with the power of preventing it; for the judge beholds them all, and judges them all in his own presence.

~ ~ ~

(Enoch 43:1)
I beheld another splendor, and the stars of heaven. I observed that he called them all by their respective names, and that they heard. In a righteous balance I saw that he weighed out with their light the amplitude of their places, and the day of their appearance, and their conversion. Splendor produced splendor; and their conversion was into the number of the angels, and of the faithful.

(Enoch 43:2)
Then I inquired of the angel, who proceeded with me, and explained to me secret things, what their names were. He answered, A similitude of those has the Lord of spirits shown you. They are names of the righteous who dwell on earth, and who believe in the name of the Lord of spirits forever and forever.

~ ~ ~

(Enoch 44)
Another thing also I saw respecting splendor; that it rises out of the stars, and becomes splendor; being incapable of forsaking them.

~ ~ ~

(Enoch 71:1)
The book of the revolutions of the luminaries of heaven, according to their respective classes, their respective powers, their respective periods, their respective names, the places where they commence their progress, and their respective months, which Uriel, the holy angel who was with me, explained to me; he who conducts them. The whole account of them, according to every year of the world forever, until a new work shall be effected, which will be eternal.

(Enoch 71:2)
This is the first law of the luminaries. The sun and the light arrive at the gates of heaven, which are on the east, and on the west of it at the western gates of heaven.

(Enoch 71:3)
I beheld the gates where the sun goes forth; and the gates where the sun sets;

(Enoch 71:4)
In which gates, the moon also rises and sets; and I beheld the conductors of the stars, among those who precede them; six gates were at the rising, and six at the setting of the sun.

(Enoch 71:5)
All these respectively, one after another, are on a level; and numerous windows are on the right and on the left sides of those gates.

(Enoch 71:6)
First proceeds forth that great luminary, which is called the sun; the orb of which is as the orb of heaven, the whole of it being replete with splendid and flaming fire.

(Enoch 71:7)
Its chariot, where it ascends, the wind blows.

(Enoch 71:8)
The sun sets in heaven, and, returning by the north, to proceed towards the east, is conducted so as to enter by that gate, and illuminate the face of heaven.

(Enoch 71:9)
In the same manner, it goes forth in the first month by a great gate.

(Enoch 71:10)
It goes forth through the fourth of those six gates, which are at the rising of the sun.

(Enoch 71:11)
And in the fourth gate, through which the sun with the moon proceeds, in the first part of it, there are twelve open windows; from which issues out a flame, when they are opened at their proper periods.

(Enoch 71:12)
When the sun rises in heaven, it goes forth through this fourth gate thirty days, and by the fourth gate in the west of heaven on a level with it descends.

(Enoch 71:13)
During that period, the day is lengthened from the day, and the night curtailed from the night for thirty days. And then the day is longer by two parts than the night.

(Enoch 71:14)
The day is precisely ten parts, and the night is eight.

(Enoch 71:15)
The sun goes forth through this fourth gate, and sets in it, and turns to the fifth gate during thirty days; after which it proceeds from, and sets in, the fifth gate.

(Enoch 71:16)
Then the day becomes lengthened by a second portion, so that it is eleven parts: while the night becomes shortened, and is only seven parts.

(Enoch 71:17)
The sun now returns to the east, entering into the sixth gate, and rising and setting in the sixth gate thirty-one days, on account of its signs.

(Enoch 71:18)
At that period, the day is longer than the night, being twice as long as the night; and becomes twelve parts;

(Enoch 71:19)
But the night is shortened, and becomes six parts. Then the sun rises up, that the day may be shortened, and the night lengthened.

(Enoch 71:20)
And the sun returns towards the east, entering into the sixth gate, where it rises and sets for thirty days.

(Enoch 71:21)
When that period is completed, the day becomes shortened precisely one part, so that it is eleven parts, while the night is seven parts.

(Enoch 71:22)
Then the sun goes from the west, from that sixth gate, and proceeds eastwards, rising in the fifth gate for thirty days, and setting again westwards in the fifth gate of the west.

(Enoch 71:23)
At that period, the day becomes shortened two parts; and is ten parts, while the night is eight parts.

(Enoch 71:24)
Then the sun goes from the fifth gate, as it sets in the fifth gate of the west; and rises in the fourth gate for thirty-one days, on account of its signs, setting in the west.

(Enoch 71:25)
At that period, the day is made equal with the night; and, being equal with it, the night becomes nine parts, and the day nine parts.

(Enoch 71:26)
Then the sun goes from that gate, as it sets in the west; and returning to the east proceeds by the third gate for thirty days, setting in the west at the third gate.

(Enoch 71:27)
At that period, the night is lengthened from the day during thirty mornings, and the day is curtailed from the day during thirty days; the night being ten parts precisely, and the day eight parts.

(Enoch 71:28)
The sun now goes from the third gate, as it sets in the third gate in the west; but returning to the east, it proceeds by the second gate of the east for thirty days.

(Enoch 71:29)
In like manner, it also sets in the second gate in the west of heaven.

(Enoch 71:30)
At that period, the night is eleven parts, and the day seven parts.

(Enoch 71:31)
Then the sun goes at that time from the second gate, as it sets in the second gate in the west; but returns to the east, proceeding by the first gate, for thirty-one days.

(Enoch 71:32)
And sets in the west in the first gate.

(Enoch 71:33)
At that period, the night is lengthened as much again as the day.

(Enoch 71:34)
It is twelve parts precisely, while the day is six parts.

(Enoch 71:35)
The sun has thus completed its beginnings, and a second time goes round from these beginnings.

(Enoch 71:36)
Into that gate it enters for thirty days, and sets in the west, in the opposite part of heaven.

(Enoch 71:37)
At that period, the night is contracted in its length a fourth part, that is, one portion, and becomes eleven parts.

(Enoch 71:38)
The day is seven parts.

(Enoch 71:39)
Then the sun returns, and enters into the second gate of the east.

(Enoch 71:40)
It returns by these beginnings thirty days, rising and setting.

(Enoch 71:41)
At that period, the night is contracted in its length. It becomes ten parts, and the day eight parts. Then the sun goes from that second gate, and sets in the west; but returns to the east, and rises in the east, in the third gate, thirty-one days, setting in the west of heaven.

(Enoch 71:42)
At that period, the night becomes shortened. It is nine parts. And the night is equal with the day. The year is precisely three hundred and sixty-four days.

(Enoch 71:43)
The lengthening of the day and night, and the contraction of the day and night, are made to differ from each other by the progress of the sun.

(Enoch 71:44)
By means of this progress the day is daily lengthened, and the night greatly shortened.

(Enoch 71:45)
This is the law and progress of the sun, and its turning when it turns back, turning during sixty days, and going forth. This

is the great everlasting luminary, that which he names the sun forever and ever.

(Enoch 71:46)
This also is that which goes forth a great luminary, and which is named after its peculiar kind, as God commanded.

(Enoch 71:47)
And thus, it goes in and out, neither slackening nor resting; but running on in its chariot by day and by night. It shines with a seventh portion of light from the moon; but the dimensions of both are equal.

~ ~ ~

(Enoch 72:1)
After this law, I beheld another law of an inferior luminary, the name of which is the moon, and the orb of which is as the orb of heaven.

(Enoch 72:2)
Its chariot, which it secretly ascends, the wind blows; and light is given to it by measure.

(Enoch 72:3)
Every month at its exit and entrance it becomes changed; and its periods are as the periods of the sun. And when in like manner its light is to exist, its light is a seventh portion from the light of the sun.

(Enoch 72:4)
Thus, it rises, and at its commencement towards the east goes forth for thirty days.

(Enoch 72:5)
At that time, it appears, and becomes to you the beginning of the month. Thirty days it is with the sun in the gate from which the sun goes forth.

(Enoch 72:6)
Half of it is in extent seven portions, one half; and the whole of its orb is void of light, except a seventh portion out of the fourteen portions of its light. And in a day, it receives a seventh portion, or half that portion, of its light. Its light is by sevens, by one portion, and by the half of a portion. It sets with the sun.

(Enoch 72:7)
And when the sun rises, the moon rises with it; receiving half a portion of light.

(Enoch 72:8)
On that night, when it commences its period, previously to the day of the month, the moon sets with the sun.

(Enoch 72:9)
And on that night, it is dark in its fourteen portions, that is, in each half; but it rises on that day with one seventh portion precisely, and in its progress declines from the rising of the sun.

(Enoch 72:10)
During the remainder of its period its light increases to fourteen portions.

~ ~ ~

(Enoch 73:1)
Then I saw another progress and regulation which he effected in the law of the moon. The progress of the moons, and everything relating to them, Uriel showed me, the holy angel who conducted them all.

(Enoch 73:2)
Their stations I wrote down as he showed them to me.

(Enoch 73:3)
I wrote down their months, as they occur, and the appearance of their light, until it is completed in fifteen days.

(Enoch 73:4)
In each of its two seven portions it completes all its light at rising and at setting.

(Enoch 73:5)
On stated months, it changes its settings; and on stated months it makes its progress through each gate. In two gates the moon sets with the sun. In those two gates which are in the midst, in the third and fourth gate. From the third gate, it goes forth for seven days, and makes its circuit.

(Enoch 73:6)
Again, it returns to the gate where the sun goes forth, and in that completes the whole of its light. Then it declines from the sun, and enters in eight days into the sixth gate, and returns in seven days to the third gate, from which the sun goes forth.

(Enoch 73:7)
When the sun proceeds to the fourth gate, the moon goes forth for seven days, until it passes from the fifth gate.

(Enoch 73:8)
Again, it returns in seven days to the fourth gate, and completing all its light, declines, and passes on by the first gate in eight days;

(Enoch 73:9)
And returns in seven days to the fourth gate, from which the sun goes forth.

(Enoch 73:10)
Thus, I beheld their stations, as according to the fixed order of the months the sun rises and sets.

(Enoch 73:11)
At those times, there is an excess of thirty days belonging to the sun in five years; all the days belonging to each year of the five years, when completed, amount to three hundred and sixty-four days; and to the sun and stars belong six days; six days in each of the five years; thus, thirty days belong to them;

(Enoch 73:12)
So that the moon has thirty days less than the sun and stars.

(Enoch 73:13)
The moon brings on all the years exactly, that their stations may come neither too forwards nor too backwards a single day; but that the years may be changed with correct precision in three hundred and sixty-four days. In three years the days are one thousand and ninety-two; in five years, they are one thousand eight hundred and twenty; and in eight years two

thousand nine hundred and twelve days.

(Enoch 73:14)
To the moon alone belong in three years one thousand and sixty-two days; in five years, it has fifty days less than the sun, for an addition being made to the one thousand and sixty-two days, in five years there are one thousand seven hundred and seventy days; and the days of the moon in eight years are two thousand eight hundred and thirty-two days.

(Enoch 73:15)
For its days in eight years are less than those of the sun by eighty days, which eighty days are its diminution in eight years.

(Enoch 73:16)
The year then becomes truly complete according to the station of the moons, and the station of the sun; which rise in the different gates; which rise and set in them for thirty days.

~ ~ ~

(Enoch 74:1)
These are the leaders of the chiefs of the thousands, those which preside over all creation, and over all the stars; with the four days which are added and never separated from the place allotted them, according to the complete computation of the year.

(Enoch 74:2)
And these serve four days, which are not computed in the computation of the year.

(Enoch 74:3)
Respecting them, men greatly err, for these luminaries truly serve, in the mansion of the world, one day in the first gate, one in the third gate, one in the fourth, and one in the sixth gate.

(Enoch 74:4)
And the harmony of the world becomes complete every three hundred and sixty-fourth state of it. For the signs,

(Enoch 74:5)
The seasons,

(Enoch 74:6)
The years,

(Enoch 74:7)
And the days, Uriel showed me; the angel whom the Lord of glory appointed over all the luminaries.

(Enoch 74:8)
Of heaven in heaven, and in the world; that they might rule in the face of the sky, and appearing over the earth, become

(Enoch 74:9)
Conductors of the days and nights: the sun, the moon, the stars, and all the ministers of heaven, which make their circuit with all the chariots of heaven.

(Enoch 74:10)
Thus, Uriel showed me twelve gates open for the circuit of the chariots of the sun in heaven, from which the rays of the sun shoot forth.

(Enoch 74:11)
From these proceed heat over the earth, when they are opened in their stated seasons. They are for the winds, and the spirit of the dew, when in their seasons they are opened; opened in heaven at its extremities.

(Enoch 74:12)
Twelve gates I beheld in heaven, at the extremities of the earth, through which the sun, moon, and stars, and all the works of heaven, proceed at their rising and setting.

(Enoch 74:13)
Many windows also are open on the right and on the left.

(Enoch 74:14)
One window at a certain season grows extremely hot. So also are there gates from which the stars go forth as they are commanded, and in which they set according to their number.

(Enoch 74:15)
I saw likewise the chariots of heaven, running in the world above to those gates in which the stars turn, which never set. One of these is greater than all, which goes round the whole world.

~ ~ ~

(Enoch 77:1)
The names of the sun are these: one Aryares, the other Tomas.

(Enoch 77:2)
The moon has four names. The first is Asonya; the second, Ebla; the third, Benase; and the fourth, Erae.

(Enoch 77:3)
These are the two great luminaries whose orbs are as the orbs of heaven; and the dimensions of both are equal.

(Enoch 77:4)
In the orb of the sun there is a seventh portion of light, which is added to it from the moon. By measure it is put in, until a seventh portion of the light of the sun is departed. They set, enter into the western gate, circuit by the north, and through the eastern gate go forth over the face of heaven.

(Enoch 77:5)
When the moon rises, it appears in heaven; and the half of a seventh portion of light is all which is in it.

(Enoch 77:6)
In fourteen days, the whole of its light is completed.

(Enoch 77:7)
By three quintuples light is put into it, until in fifteen days its light is completed, according to the signs of the year; it has three quintuples.

(Enoch 77:8)
The moon has the half of a seventh portion.

(Enoch 77:9)
During its diminution on the first day its light decreases a fourteenth part; on the second day it decreases a thirteenth part; on the third day a twelfth part; on the fourth day an

eleventh part; on the fifth day a tenth part; on the sixth day a ninth part; on the seventh day it decreases an eighth part; on the eighth day it decreases a seventh part; on the ninth day it decreases a sixth part; on the tenth day it decreases a fifth part; on the eleventh day it decreases a fourth part; on the twelfth day it decreases a third part; on the thirteenth day it decreases a second part; on the fourteenth day it decreases a half of its seventh part; and on the fifteenth day the whole remainder of its light is consumed.

(Enoch 77:10)
On stated months, the moon has twenty-nine days.

(Enoch 77:11)
It also has a period of twenty-eight days.

(Enoch 77:12)
Uriel likewise showed me another regulation, when light is poured into the moon, how it is poured into it from the sun.

(Enoch 77:13)
All the time that the moon is in progress with its light, it is poured into it in the presence of the sun, until its light is in fourteen days completed in heaven.

(Enoch 77:14)
And when it is wholly extinguished, its light is consumed in heaven; and on the first day it is called the new moon, for on that day light is received into it.

(Enoch 77:15)
It becomes precisely completed on the day that the sun descends into the west, while the moon ascends at night from the east.

(Enoch 77:16)
The moon then shines all the night, until the sun rises before it; when the moon disappears in turn before the sun.

(Enoch 77:17)
Where light comes to the moon, there again it decreases, until all its light is extinguished, and the days of the moon pass away.

(Enoch 77:18)
Then its orb remains solitary without light.

(Enoch 77:19)
During three months, it effects in thirty days each month its period; and during three more months it effects it in twenty-nine days each. These are the times in which it effects its decrease in its first period, and in the first gate, namely, in one hundred and seventy-seven days.

(Enoch 77:20)
And at the time of its going forth during three months it appears thirty days each, and during three more months it appears twenty-nine days each.

(Enoch 77:21)
In the night, it appears for each twenty days as the face of a man, and in the day as heaven; for it is nothing else except its light.

~ ~ ~

(Enoch 78:1)
And now, my son Mathusala, I have shown you everything; and the account of every ordinance of the stars of heaven is finished.

(Enoch 78:2)
He showed me every ordinance respecting these, which takes place at all times and in all seasons under every influence, in all years, at the arrival and under the rule of each, during every month and every week. He showed me also the decrease of the moon, which is effected in the sixth gate; for in that sixth gate is its light consumed.

(Enoch 78:3)
From this is the beginning of the month; and its decrease is effected in the sixth gate in its period, until a hundred and seventy-seven days are completed; according to the mode of computation by weeks, twenty-five weeks and two days.

(Enoch 78:4)
Its period is less than that of the sun, according to the ordinance of the stars, by five days in one half year precisely.

(Enoch 78:5)
When that their visible situation is completed. Such is the appearance and likeness of every luminary, which Thiel, the great angel who conducts them, showed to me.

~ ~ ~

(Enoch 79:1)
In those days Uriel answered and said to me, Behold, I have

showed you all things, O Enoch.

(Enoch 79:2)
And all things have I revealed to you. You see the sun, the moon, and those which conduct the stars of heaven, which cause all their operations, seasons, and arrivals to return.

(Genesis 1:20)
And God said, Let the waters bring forth abundantly the moving creature that has life, and birds that may fly above the earth in the open firmament of heaven.

(Genesis 1:21) (...Jubilees 2:11)
And on the fifth day God created great sea monsters in the depths of the waters, for these were the first things of flesh that were created by His hands, the fish and every living creature that moves in the waters, which the waters brought forth abundantly, after their kind, and everything that flies, and every winged bird after his kind. And God saw that it was good.

(Genesis 1:22)
And God blessed them, saying, Be fruitful, and multiply, and fill the waters in the seas, and let birds multiply in the earth.

(Jubilees 2:12)
And the sun rose above them to prosper them, and above everything that was on the earth, everything that shoots out of the earth, and all fruit-bearing trees, and all flesh.

(Genesis 1:23) (Jubilees 2:13...)
These three kinds He created, and the evening and the morning were the fifth day.

(Genesis 1:24)

And God said, Let the earth bring forth the living creature after his kind, cattle, and creeping thing, and beast of the earth after his kind: and it was so.

(Genesis 1:25) (...Jubilees 2:13)

And on the sixth day, God made all the animals of the earth after his kind, and all cattle after their kind, and everything that moves on the earth after his kind. And God saw that it was good.

(Genesis 1:26) (Jasher 1:1...)

And God said, Let us make man in our image, after our likeness: and let them have dominion over the fish of the sea, and over the birds of the air, and over the cattle, and over all the earth, and over every creeping thing that creeps on the earth.

(Genesis 1:27) (...Jasher 1:1) (Jubilees 2:14...)

And after all this God created man in His own image, He created him in the image of God; He created them male and female, a man and a woman.

(Genesis 1:28) (Jasher 1:6...)

And God blessed them, and the Lord God said to them, Be fruitful, and multiply, and fill the earth, and subdue it: and have dominion over the fish of the sea, and over the birds of the air, and over every living thing that moves on the earth.

(...Jubilees 2:14)

And God gave him dominion over all that is on the earth, and in the seas, and over everything that flies, and over beasts and over cattle, and over everything that moves on the earth, and over the whole earth, and over all this He gave him dominion.

(Genesis 1:29)

And God said, Behold, I have given you every herb bearing seed, which is on the face of all the earth, and every tree, in which is the fruit of a tree yielding seed; to you it shall be for meat.

(Genesis 1:30)

And to every beast of the earth, and to every bird of the air, and to everything that creeps on the earth, wherein there is life, I have given every green herb for meat: and it was so.

(Jubilees 2:15)

And these four kinds He created on the sixth day. And there were altogether two and twenty kinds.

(Jubilees 2:16)

And He finished all his work on the sixth day - all that is in the heavens and on the earth, and in the seas and in the abysses, and in the light and in the darkness, and in everything.

(Jasher 1:8)

And when God had blessed them and commanded them, He went from them, and Adam and his wife dwelt in the garden according to the command which the Lord had commanded them.

(Genesis 1:31)

And God saw everything that he had made, and, behold, it was very good. And the evening and the morning were the sixth day.

Genesis: Chapter Two

(Genesis 2:1)
Thus, the heavens and the earth were finished, and all the host of them.

(Enoch 3:1)
All who are in the heavens know what is transacted there.

(Enoch 3:2)
They know that the heavenly luminaries change not their paths; that each rises and sets regularly, everyone at its proper period, without transgressing the commands which they have received. They behold the earth, and understand what is there transacted, from the beginning to the end of it.

(Enoch 3:3)
They see that every work of God is invariable in the period of its appearance. They behold summer and winter: perceiving that the whole earth is full of water; and that the cloud, the dew, and the rain refresh it.

~ ~ ~

(Enoch 4)
They consider and behold every tree, how it appears to wither, and every leaf to fall off, except of fourteen trees, which are not deciduous; which wait from the old, to the appearance of the new leaf, for two or three winters.

(Enoch 5)
Again, they consider the days of summer, that the sun is on it at its very beginning; while you seek for a covered and shady spot on account of the burning sun; while the earth is scorched up with fervid heat, and you become incapable of walking either on the ground or on the rocks in consequence of that heat.

~ ~ ~

(Genesis 2:2)

And on the seventh day God ended his work which He had made; and He rested on the seventh day from all His work which He had made.

(Genesis 2:3)

And God blessed the seventh day, and sanctified it: because that in it He had rested from all His work which God created and made.

(Jubilees 2:17)
And He gave us a great sign, the Sabbath day, that we should work six days, but keep Sabbath on the seventh day from all work.

(Jubilees 2:18)
And all the angels of the presence, and all the angels of sanctification, these two great classes - He has bidden us to keep the Sabbath with Him in heaven and on earth.

(Jubilees 2:19)
And He said to us: Behold, I will separate to Myself a people

from among all the peoples, and these shall keep the Sabbath day, and I will sanctify them to Myself as My people, and will bless them; as I have sanctified the Sabbath day and do sanctify to Myself, even so will I bless them, and they shall be My people and I will be their God.

(Jubilees 2:20)
And I have chosen the seed of Jacob from among all that I have seen, and have written him down as My first-born son, and have sanctified him to Myself forever and ever; and I will teach them the Sabbath day, that they may keep Sabbath thereon from all work.

(Jubilees 2:21)
And thus He created therein a sign in accordance with which they should keep Sabbath with us on the seventh day, to eat and to drink, and to bless Him who has created all things as He has blessed and sanctified to Himself a peculiar people above all peoples, and that they should keep Sabbath together with us.

(Jubilees 2:22)
And He caused His commands to ascend as a sweet savor acceptable before Him all the days . . .

(Jubilees 2:23)
There were two and twenty heads of mankind from Adam to Jacob, and two and twenty kinds of work were made until the seventh day; this is blessed and holy; and the former also is blessed and holy; and this one serves with that one for sanctification and blessing.

(Jubilees 2:24)
And to this it was granted that they should always be the

blessed and holy ones of the first testimony and law, even as He had sanctified and blessed the Sabbath day on the seventh day.

(Jubilees 2:25)
He created heaven and earth and everything that He created in six days, and God made the seventh day holy, for all His works; therefore He commanded on its behalf that, whoever does any work thereon shall die, and that he who defiles it shall surely die.

(Jubilees 2:26)
Wherefore do you command the children of Israel to observe this day that they may keep it holy and not do thereon any work, and not to defile it, as it is holier than all other days.

(Jubilees 2:27)
And whoever profanes it shall surely die, and whoever does thereon any work shall surely die eternally, that the children of Israel may observe this day throughout their generations, and not be rooted out of the land; for it is a holy day and a blessed day.

(Jubilees 2:28)
And everyone who observes it and keeps Sabbath thereon from all his work, will be holy and blessed throughout all days like to us.

(Jubilees 2:29)
Declare and say to the children of Israel the law of this day both that they should keep Sabbath thereon, and that they should not forsake it in the error of their hearts; that it is not lawful to do any work thereon which is unseemly, to do thereon their own pleasure, and that they should not prepare

thereon anything to be eaten or drunk, and (that it is not lawful) to draw water, or bring in or take out thereon through their gates any burden, which they had not prepared for themselves on the sixth day in their dwellings.

(Jubilees 2:30)
And they shall not bring in nor take out from house to house on that day; for that day is more holy and blessed than any jubilee day of the jubilees; on this we kept Sabbath in the heavens before it was made known to any flesh to keep Sabbath thereon on the earth.

(Jubilees 2:31)
And the Creator of all things blessed it, but he did not sanctify all peoples and nations to keep Sabbath thereon, but Israel alone: them alone he permitted to eat and drink and to keep Sabbath thereon on the earth.

(Jubilees 2:32)
And the Creator of all things blessed this day which He had created for blessing and holiness and glory above all days.

(Jubilees 2:33)
This law and testimony was given to the children of Israel as a law forever to their generations.

~ ~ ~

(Jubilees 50:6)
And behold the commandment regarding the Sabbaths - I have written (them) down for you - and all the judgments of its laws.

(Jubilees 50:7)
Six days shall you labor, but on the seventh day is the Sabbath of the Lord your God. In it you shall do no manner of work, you and your sons, and your men- servants and your maid-servants, and all your cattle and the sojourner also who is with you.

(Jubilees 50:8)
And the man that does any work on it shall die: whoever desecrates that day, whoever lies with his wife, or whoever says he will do something on it, that he will set out on a journey thereon in regard to any buying or selling: and whoever draws water thereon which he had not prepared for himself on the sixth day, and whoever takes up any burden to carry it out of his tent or out of his house shall die.

(Jubilees 50:9)
You shall do no work whatever on the Sabbath day save what you have prepared for yourselves on the sixth day, so as to eat, and drink, and rest, and keep Sabbath from all work on that day, and to bless the Lord your God, who has given you a day of festival and a holy day: and a day of the holy kingdom for all Israel is this day among their days forever.

(Jubilees 50:10)
For great is the honor which the Lord has given to Israel that they should eat and drink and be satisfied on this festival day, and rest thereon from all labor which belongs to the labor of the children of men save burning frankincense and bringing oblations and sacrifices before the Lord for days and for Sabbaths.

(Jubilees 50:11)
This work alone shall be done on the Sabbath - days in the sanctuary of the Lord your God; that they may atone for Israel

with sacrifice continually from day to day for a memorial well-pleasing before the Lord, and that He may receive them always from day to day according as you have been commanded.

(Jubilees 50:12)
And every man who does any work thereon, or goes a journey, or tills his farm, whether in his house or any other place, and whoever lights a fire, or rides on any beast, or travels by ship on the sea, and whoever strikes or kills anything, or slaughters a beast or a bird, or whoever catches an animal or a bird or a fish, or whoever fasts or makes war on the Sabbaths:

(Jubilees 50:13)
The man who does any of these things on the Sabbath shall die, so that the children of Israel shall observe the Sabbaths according to the commandments regarding the Sabbaths of the land, as it is written in the tablets, which He gave into my hands that I should write out for you the laws of the seasons, and the seasons according to the division of their days.

(Genesis 2:4)

These are the generations of the heavens and of the earth when they were created, in the day that the Lord God made the earth and the heavens,

(Enoch 33:1)
From there I advanced on towards the north, to the extremities of the earth.

(Enoch 33:2)
And there I saw a great and glorious wonder at the extremities of the whole earth.

(Enoch 33:3)
There I saw heavenly gates opening into heaven; three of them distinctly separated. The northern winds proceeded from them, blowing cold, hail, frost, snow, dew, and rain.

(Enoch 33:4)
From one of the gates they blew mildly; but when they blew from the two other gates, it was with violence and force. They blew over the earth strongly.

~ ~ ~

(Enoch 34:1)
From there I went to the extremities of the world westwards;

(Enoch 34:2)
Where I perceived three gates open, as I had seen in the north; the gates and passages through them being of equal magnitude.

~ ~ ~

(Enoch 35:1)
Then I proceeded to the extremities of the earth southwards; where I saw three gates open to the south, from which issued dew, rain, and wind.

(Enoch 35:2)
From there I went to the extremities of heaven eastwards;

where I saw three heavenly gates open to the east, which had smaller gates within them. Through each of these small gates the stars of heaven passed on, and proceeded towards the west by a path which was seen by them, and that at every period of their appearance.

(Enoch 35:3)
When I beheld them, I blessed; every time in which they appeared, I blessed the Lord of glory, who had made those great and splendid signs, that they might display the magnificence of his works to angels and to the souls of men; and that these might glorify all his works and operations; might see the effect of his power; might glorify the great labor of his hands; and bless him forever.

~ ~ ~

(Enoch 41:1)
After this I beheld the secrets of the heavens and of paradise, according to its divisions; and of human action, as they weigh it there in balances. I saw the habitations of the elect, and the habitations of the holy. And there my eyes beheld all the sinners, who denied the Lord of glory, and whom they were expelling from there, and dragging away, as they stood there; no punishment proceeding against them from the Lord of spirits.

(Enoch 41:2)
There, too, my eyes beheld the secrets of the lightning and the thunder; and the secrets of the winds, how they are distributed as they blow over the earth: the secrets of the winds, of the dew, and of the clouds. There I perceived the place from

which they issued forth, and became saturated with the dust of the earth.

(Enoch 41:3)
There I saw the wooden receptacles out of which the winds became separated, the receptacle of hail, the receptacle of snow, the receptacle of the clouds, and the cloud itself, which continued over the earth before the creation of the world.

~ ~ ~

(Enoch 42:1)
Wisdom found not a place on earth where she could inhabit; her dwelling therefore is in heaven.

(Enoch 42:2)
Wisdom went forth to dwell among the sons of men, but she obtained not a habitation. Wisdom returned to her place, and seated herself in the midst of the angels. But iniquity went forth after her return, who unwillingly found a habitation, and resided among them, as rain in the desert, and as a dew in a thirsty land.

~ ~ ~

(Enoch 59:1)
Then another angel, who proceeded with me, spoke to me;

(Enoch 59:2)
And showed me the first and last secrets in heaven above, and in the depths of the earth:

(Enoch 59:3)
In the extremities of heaven, and in the foundations of it, and in the receptacle of the winds.

(Enoch 59:4)
He showed me how their spirits were divided; how they were balanced; and how both the springs and the winds were numbered according to the force of their spirit.

(Enoch 59:5)
He showed me the power of the moon's light, that its power is a just one; as well as the divisions of the stars, according to their respective names;

(Enoch 59:6)
That every division is divided; that the lightning flashes;

(Enoch 59:7)
That its troops immediately obey; and that a cessation takes place during thunder in continuance of its sound. Nor are the thunder and the lightning separated; neither do both of them move with one spirit; yet are they not separated.

(Enoch 59:8)
For when the lightning lightens, the thunder sounds, and the spirit at a proper period pauses, making an equal division between them; for the receptacle, on which their periods depend, is loose as sand. Each of them at a proper season is restrained with a bridle; and turned by the power of the spirit,

which thus propels them according to the spacious extent of the earth.

(Enoch 59:9)
The spirit likewise of the sea is potent and strong; and as a strong power causes it to ebb, so is it driven forwards, and scattered against the mountains of the earth. The spirit of the frost has its angel; in the spirit of hail there is a good angel; the spirit of snow ceases in its strength, and a solitary spirit is in it, which ascends from it like vapor, and is called refrigeration.

(Enoch 59:10)
The spirit also of mist dwells with them in their receptacle; but it has a receptacle to itself; for its progress is in splendor,

(Enoch 59:11)
In light, and in darkness, in winter and in summer. It receptacle is bright, and an angel is in it.

(Enoch 59:12)
The spirit of dew has its abode in the extremities of heaven, in connection with the receptacle of rain; and its progress is in winter and in summer. The cloud produced by it, and the cloud of the mist, become united; one gives to the other; and when the spirit of rain is in motion from its receptacle, angels come, and opening its receptacle, bring it forth.

(Enoch 59:13)
When likewise, it is sprinkled over all the earth, it forms an union with every kind of water on the ground; for the waters remain on the ground, because they afford nourishment to the earth from the Most High, who is in heaven.

(Enoch 59:14)
On this account, therefore, there is a regulation in the quantity of rain, which the angels receive.

(Enoch 59:15)
These things I saw; all of them, even paradise.

~ ~ ~

(Enoch 68:19)
This is the number of the Kesbel; the principal part of the oath which the Most High, dwelling in glory, revealed to the holy ones.

(Enoch 68:20)
Its name is Beka. He spoke to holy Michael to discover to them the sacred name, that they might understand that secret name, and thus remember the oath; and that those who pointed out every secret thing to the children of men might tremble at that name and oath.

(Enoch 68:21)
This is the power of that oath; for powerful it is, and strong.

(Enoch 68:22)
And he established this oath of Akae by the instrumentality of the holy Michael.

(Enoch 68:23)
These are the secrets of this oath, and by it were they confirmed.

(Enoch 68:24)
Heaven was suspended by it before the world was made, forever.

(Enoch 68:25)
By it has the earth been founded on the flood; while from the concealed parts of the hills the agitated waters proceed forth from the creation to the end of the world.

(Enoch 68:26)
By this oath the sea has been formed, and the foundation of it.

(Enoch 68:27)
During the period of its fury he has established the sand against it, which continues unchanged forever; and by this oath the abyss has been made strong; nor is it removable from its station forever and ever.

(Enoch 68:28)
By this oath the sun and moon complete their progress, never swerving from the command given to them forever and ever.

(Enoch 68:29)
By this oath the stars complete their progress;

(Enoch 68:30)
And when their names are called, they return an answer, forever and ever.

(Enoch 68:31)
Thus, the blowing of the winds take place in the heavens: all of them have breathings, and effect a complete combination of breathings.

(Enoch 68:32)
There the treasures of thunder are kept, and the splendor of the lightning.

(Enoch 68:33)
There are kept the treasures of hail and of frost, the treasures of snow, the treasures of rain and of dew.

(Enoch 68:34)
All these confess and laud before the Lord of spirits.

(Enoch 68:35)
They glorify with all their power of praise; and he sustains them in all that act of thanksgiving; while they laud, glorify, and exalt the name of the Lord of spirits forever and ever.

(Enoch 68:36)
And with them he establishes this oath, by which they and their paths are preserved; nor does their progress perish.

(Enoch 68:37)
Great was their joy.

(Enoch 68:38)
They blessed, glorified, and exalted, because the name of the Son of Man was revealed to them.

(Enoch 68:39)
He sat on the throne of his glory; and the principal part of the judgment was assigned to him, the Son of Man. Sinners shall disappear and perish from the face of the earth, while those who seduced them shall be bound with chains forever.

(Enoch 68:40)
According to their ranks of corruption shall they be imprisoned, and all their works shall disappear from the face of the earth; nor from there on out shall there be any to corrupt; for the Son of Man has been seen, sitting on the throne of his glory.

(Enoch 68:41)
Everything wicked shall disappear, and depart from before his face; and the word of the Son of Man shall become powerful in the presence of the Lord of spirits.

(Enoch 68:42)
This is the third parable of Enoch.

(Genesis 2:5)
And every plant of the field before it was in the earth, and every herb of the field before it grew: for the Lord God had not caused it to rain on the earth, and there was not a man to till the ground.

(Genesis 2:6)
But there went up a mist from the earth, and watered the whole face of the ground.

(Genesis 2:7) (Jasher 1:2)
And the Lord God formed man of the dust of the ground, and breathed into his nostrils the breath of life; and man became a living soul endowed with speech.

(Genesis 2:8)
And the Lord God planted a garden eastward in Eden; and there He put the man whom He had formed.

(Genesis 2:9)
And out of the ground the Lord God made to grow every tree that is pleasant to the sight, and good for food; the tree of life also in the midst of the garden, and the tree of knowledge of good and evil.

(Enoch 31:1)
After these things, surveying the entrances of the north, above the mountains, I perceived seven mountains replete with pure nard, odoriferous trees, cinnamon and papyrus.

(Enoch 31:2)
From there I passed on above the summits of those mountains to some distance eastwards, and went over the Erythræan Sea. And when I was advanced far beyond it, I passed along above the angel Zateel, and arrived at the garden of righteousness. In this garden I beheld, among other trees, some which were numerous and large, and which flourished there.

(Enoch 31:3)
Their fragrance was agreeable and powerful, and their appearance both varied and elegant. The tree of knowledge also was there, of which if any one eats, he becomes endowed with great wisdom.

(Enoch 31:4)
It was like a species of the tamarind tree, bearing fruit which resembled grapes extremely fine; and its fragrance extended to a considerable distance. I exclaimed, how beautiful is this tree, and how delightful is its appearance!

(Enoch 31:5)
Then holy Raphael, an angel who was with me, answered and said, This is the tree of knowledge, of which your ancient father

and your aged mother ate, who were before you; and who, obtaining knowledge, their eyes being opened, and knowing themselves to be naked, were expelled from the garden.

(Genesis 2:10)

And a river went out of Eden to water the garden; and from there it was parted, and became into four heads.

(Genesis 2:11)

The name of the first is Pison: that is it which compasses the whole land of Havilah, where there is gold;

(Genesis 2:12)

And the gold of that land is good: there is bdellium and the onyx stone.

(Genesis 2:13)

And the name of the second river is Gihon: the same is it that compasses the whole land of Ethiopia.

(Genesis 2:14)

And the name of the third river is Hiddekel: that is it which goes toward the east of Assyria. And the fourth river is Euphrates.

(Genesis 2:15) (Jasher 1:7...)

And the Lord God took the man, Adam and his wife, and put him in the Garden of Eden to dress it and to keep it.

(Genesis 2:16) (...Jasher 1:7...)

And the Lord God commanded the man, saying, Of every tree of the garden you may freely eat:

(Genesis 2:17) (...Jasher 1:7)

But of the tree of the knowledge of good and evil, you shall not eat of it: for in the day that you eat thereof you shall surely die.

(Genesis 2:18) (Jasher 1:3) (Jubilees 3:4)

And the Lord God said to us, It is not good that the man should be alone; I will make a help meet for him.

(Genesis 2:19) (Jubilees 3:1)

And out of the ground the Lord God formed every beast of the field, and every bird of the air. And on the six days of the second week we brought them, according to the word of God, to Adam, all the beasts, and all the cattle, and all the birds, and everything that moves on the earth, and everything that moves in the water, according to their kinds, and according to their types: the beasts on the first day; the cattle on the second day; the birds on the third day; and all that which moves on the earth on the fourth day; and that which moves in the water on the fifth day, to see what he would call them:

(...Genesis 2:19) (Jubilees 3:2)

Adam named them all by their respective names and whatsoever Adam called every living creature, that was the name thereof.

(Genesis 2:20) (Jubilees 3:3)

And Adam gave names to all cattle, and to the birds of the air, and to every beast of the field; And on these five days Adam saw all these, male and female, according to every kind that was on the earth, but he was alone and for Adam there was not found a help meet for him.

(Genesis 2:21) (Jasher 1:4...) (Jubilees 3:5)

And the Lord our God caused a deep sleep to fall on Adam,

and he slept: and He took for the woman one of his ribs from among his ribs, and closed up the flesh thereof;

(Genesis 2:22) (...Jasher 1:4) (Jubilees 3:5,6...)
And the rib, which the Lord God had taken from man, was the origin of the woman from among his ribs, He built flesh on it, and formed it -- He made a woman, and brought her to Adam, the man. And He woke up Adam out of his sleep and Adam awoke from his sleep, and on awaking, he rose on the sixth day, and behold a woman was standing before him.

(Genesis 2:23) (Jasher 1:5...) (...Jubilees 3:6)
And he knew her, and Adam said, This is now bone of my bones, and flesh of my flesh: she shall be called Woman, because she was taken out of Man.

(Genesis 2:24) (Jubilees 3:7)
Therefore, shall man and wife be one and a man shall leave his father and his mother, and shall cleave to his wife: and they shall be one flesh.

(Genesis 2:25)
And they were both naked, the man and his wife, and were not ashamed.

(Jubilees 3:8)
In the first week was Adam created, and the rib - his wife: in the second week He showed her to him: and for this reason the commandment was given to keep in their defilement, for a male seven days, and for a female twice seven days.

(Jubilees 3:9)
And after Adam had completed forty days in the land where he had been created, we brought him into the Garden of Eden

to till and keep it, but his wife they brought in on the eightieth day, and after this she entered into the Garden of Eden.

(Jubilees 3:10)
And for this reason, the commandment is written on the heavenly tablets in regard to her that gives birth: if she bears a male, she shall remain in her uncleanness seven days according to the first week of days, and thirty and three days shall she remain in the blood of her purifying, and she shall not touch any hallowed thing, nor enter into the sanctuary, until she accomplishes these days which are enjoined in the case of a male child.

(Jubilees 3:11)
But in the case of a female child she shall remain in her uncleanness two weeks of days, according to the first two weeks, and sixty-six days in the blood of her purification, and they will be in all eighty days.

(Jubilees 3:12)
And when she had completed these eighty days we brought her into the Garden of Eden, for it is holier than all the earth besides and every tree that is planted in it is holy.

(Jubilees 3:13)
Therefore, there was ordained regarding her who bears a male or a female child the statute of those days that she should touch no hallowed thing, nor enter into the sanctuary until these days for the male or female child are accomplished.

(Jubilees 3:14)
This is the law and testimony which was written down for Israel, in order that they should observe it all the days.

(Jubilees 3:15)
And in the first week of the first jubilee, Adam and his wife were in the Garden of Eden for seven years tilling and keeping it, and we gave him work and we instructed him to do everything that is suitable for tillage.

(Jubilees 3:16)
And he tilled the garden, and was naked and knew it not, and was not ashamed, and he protected the garden from the birds and beasts and cattle, and gathered its fruit, and eat, and put aside the residue for himself and for his wife [and put aside that which was being kept].

Genesis: Chapter Three

(Genesis 3:1) (Jasher 1:9) (Jubilees 3:17)

And after the completion of the seven years, which he had completed there, seven years exactly, and in the second month, on the seventeenth day, the serpent, which God had created with them in the earth, was more subtil than any beast of the field which the Lord God had made, came to them, and appraoched the woman to incite them to transgress the command of God which he had commanded them. And the serpent said to the woman, Yea, has God said, You shall not eat of every tree of the garden?

(Genesis 3:2) (Jubilees 3:18...)

And the woman said to the serpent, God has said to us we may eat of the fruit of the trees of the garden:

(Genesis 3:3) (...Jubilees 3:18)

But of the fruit of the tree which is in the midst of the garden, God has said to us, You shall not eat of it, neither shall you touch it, lest you die.

(Genesis 3:4) (Jubilees 3:19...)

And the serpent said to the woman, You shall not surely die:

(Genesis 3:5) (...Jubilees 3:19)

For God knows that in the day you eat thereof, then your eyes shall be opened, and you shall be as gods, knowing good and evil.

(Jasher 1:10...)
And the serpent enticed and persuaded the woman to eat from the tree of knowledge...

(Genesis 3:6) (...Jasher 1:10) (Jubilees 3:20, 21...)
And when the woman saw that the tree was agreeable, and that its fruit was good for food, and that it was pleasant to the eyes, and a tree to be desired to make one wise, the woman hearkened to the voice of the serpent, and she transgressed the word of God, and she took of the fruit thereof from the tree of the knowledge of good and evil, and ate. And when she had first covered her shame with fig leaves, she took from it and gave also to Adam, her husband with her; and he ate.

(Genesis 3:7) (...Jubilees 3:21, 22)
And the eyes of them both were opened, and they knew that they were naked; and they took and sewed fig leaves together, and made themselves aprons and covered his shame.

(Genesis 3:8)
And they heard the voice of the Lord God walking in the garden in the cool of the day: and Adam and his wife hid themselves from the presence of the Lord God among the trees of the garden.

(Genesis 3:9)
And the Lord God called to Adam, and said to him, Where are you?

(Genesis 3:10)
And he said, I heard your voice in the garden, and I was afraid, because I was naked; and I hid myself.

(Jasher 1:11)
And Adam and his wife transgressed the command of God which he commanded them, and God knew it and His anger was kindled against them and he cursed them.

(Genesis 3:11)

And he said, Who told you that you were naked? Have you eaten of the tree, of which I commanded you that you should not eat?

(Genesis 3:12)

And the man said, The woman whom you gave to be with me, she gave me of the tree, and I ate.

(Genesis 3:13)

And the Lord God said to the woman, What is this that you have done? And the woman said, The serpent beguiled me, and I ate.

(Jubilees 3:23)
And God cursed the serpent, and was wroth with it forever.

(Genesis 3:14)

And the Lord God said to the serpent, Because you have done this, you are cursed above all cattle, and above every beast of the field; on your belly shall you go, and dust shall you eat all the days of your life:

(Genesis 3:15)

And I will put enmity between you and the woman, and between your seed and her seed; it shall bruise your head, and you shall bruise his heel.

(Jubilees 3:24...)
And He was wroth with the woman, because she harkened to the voice of the serpent, and ate.

(Genesis 3:16) (...Jubilees 3:24)
To the woman he said, I will greatly multiply your sorrow and your conception and your pains; in sorrow you shall bring forth children; and your desire shall be to your husband, and he shall rule over you.

(Genesis 3:17) (Jubilees 3:25...)
And to Adam he said, Because you have hearkened to the voice of your wife, and have eaten of the tree, of which I commanded you, saying, You shall not eat of it: cursed is the ground for your sake; in sorrow shall you eat of it all the days of your life;

(Genesis 3:18) (...Jubilees 3:25...)
Thorns also and thistles shall it bring forth to you; and you shall eat the herb of the field;

(Genesis 3:19) (...Jubilees 3:25)
In the sweat of your face shall you eat bread, till you return to the ground; for out of it you were taken: for dust you are, and to dust you shall return.

(Genesis 3:20) (Jasher 1:5) (Jubilees 3:33)
And Adam called his wife's name Eve; because she was the mother of all living.

(Genesis 3:21) (Jubilees 3:26...)
To Adam also and to his wife the Lord God made coats of skins, and clothed them.

(Genesis 3:22)

And the Lord God said, Behold, the man is become as one of us, to know good and evil: and now, lest he put forth his hand, and take also of the tree of life, and eat, and live forever:

(Genesis 3:23) (...Jubilees 3:26)

Therefore, the Lord God sent him forth from the Garden of Eden, to till the ground from where he was taken.

(Genesis 3:24) (Jasher 1:12...)

So the Lord God, He drove out the man that day from the Garden of Eden, to till the ground from which they were taken, and they went and dwelt at the east of the Garden of Eden; and He placed at the east of the Garden of Eden Cherubims, and a flaming sword which turned every way, to keep the way of the Tree of Life.

~ ~ ~

(Enoch 24:1)

I went from there to another place, and saw a mountain of fire flashing both by day and night. I proceeded towards it; and perceived seven splendid mountains, which were all different from each other.

(Enoch 24:2)

Their stones were brilliant and beautiful; all were brilliant and splendid to behold; and beautiful was their surface. Three mountains were towards the east, and strengthened by being placed one on another; and three were towards the south, strengthened in a similar manner. There were likewise deep valleys, which did not approach each other. And the seventh mountain was in the midst of them. In length, they all resembled the seat of a throne, and odoriferous trees surrounded them.

(Enoch 24:3)
Among these there was a tree of an unceasing smell; nor of those which were in Eden was there one of all the fragrant trees which smelt like this. Its leaf, its flower, and its bark never withered, and its fruit was beautiful.

(Enoch 24:4)
Its fruit resembled the cluster of the palm. I exclaimed, behold! This tree is goodly in aspect, pleasing in its leaf, and the sight of its fruit is delightful to the eye. Then Michael, one of the holy and glorious angels who were with me, and one who presided over them, answered,

(Enoch 24:5)
And said: Enoch, why do you inquire respecting the odor of this tree?

(Enoch 24:6)
Why are you inquisitive to know it?

(Enoch 24:7)
Then I, Enoch, replied to him, and said, Concerning everything I am desirous of instruction, but particularly concerning this tree.

(Enoch 24:8)
He answered me, saying, That mountain which you behold, the extent of whose head resembles the seat of the Lord, will be the seat on which shall sit the holy and great Lord of glory,

the Everlasting King, when he shall come and descend to visit the earth with goodness.

(Enoch 24:9)
And that tree of an agreeable smell, not one of carnal odor, there shall be no power to touch, until the period of the great judgment. When all shall be punished and consumed forever, this shall be bestowed on the righteous and humble. The fruit of this tree shall be given to the elect. For towards the north life shall be planted in the holy place, towards the habitation of the Everlasting King.

(Enoch 24:10)
Then shall they greatly rejoice and exult in the holy one. The sweet odor shall enter into their bones; and they shall live a long life on the earth, as your forefathers have lived; neither in their days shall sorrow, distress, trouble, and punishment afflict them.

(Enoch 24:11)
And I blessed the Lord of glory, the Everlasting King, because he has prepared this tree for the saints, formed it, and declared that he would give it to them.

~ ~ ~

(Jubilees 3:27)
And on that day on which Adam went forth from the Garden, he offered as a sweet savor an offering, frankincense, galbanum, and stacte, and spices in the morning with the rising of the sun from the day when he covered his shame.

(Jubilees 3:28)
And on that day was closed the mouth of all beasts, and of cattle, and of birds, and of whatever walks, and of whatever moves, so that they could no longer speak: for they had all spoken one with another with one lip and with one tongue.

(Jubilees 3:29)
And He sent out of the Garden of Eden all flesh that was in the Garden of Eden, and all flesh was scattered according to its kinds, and according to its types to the places which had been created for them.

(Jubilees 3:30)
And to Adam alone He gave to cover his shame, of all the beasts and cattle.

(Jubilees 3:31)
On this account, it is prescribed on the heavenly tablets as touching all those who know the judgment of the law, that they should cover their shame, and should not uncover themselves as the Gentiles uncover themselves.

(Jubilees 3:32)
And on the new moon of the fourth month, Adam and his wife went forth from the Garden of Eden, and they dwelt in the land of Elda in the land of their creation.

(Jubilees 3:34)
And they had no son till the first jubilee, and after this he knew her.

(Jubilees 3:35)
Now he tilled the land as he had been instructed in the Garden of Eden.

Genesis: Chapter Four

(Genesis 4:1) (...Jasher 1:12, 13) (Jubilees 4:1...)

And Adam knew Eve his wife; and she conceived, and she bore two sons and three daughters. And in the third week in the second jubilee, she gave birth and she called the name of the firstborn Cain, and said, I have gotten a man from the Lord.

(Genesis 4:2) (Jasher 1:13, 14) (...Jubilees 4:1,2)

And in the fourth, she again bore his brother. And the name of the other she called Abel, for she said, In vanity we came into the earth, and in vanity we shall be taken from it. And in the fifth, she gave birth to her daughter Âwân. And the boys grew up and their father gave them a possession in the land; And Abel was a keeper of sheep, but Cain was a tiller of the ground.

(Genesis 4:3) (Jasher 1:15...)

And in process of time, it was at the expiration of a few years, it came to pass, that they brought an approximating offering to the Lord, Cain brought of the fruit of the ground an offering to the Lord.

(Genesis 4:4) (...Jasher 1:15)

And Abel, he also brought of the firstlings of his flock and of the fat thereof. And the Lord had respect to Abel and to his offering: and God turned and inclined to Abel and his offering, and a fire came down from the Lord from heaven and consumed it.

(Genesis 4:5) (Jasher 1:16)

But to Cain and to his offering the Lord did not turn, He had not respect. He did not incline to it, for he had brought from the inferior fruit of the ground before the Lord, And Cain was very wroth, and his countenance fell. And Cain was jealous against his brother Abel on account of this, and he sought a pretext to slay him.

(Genesis 4:6)

And the Lord said to Cain, Why are you wroth? And why is your countenance fallen?

(Genesis 4:7)

If you do well, shall you not be accepted? And if you do not do well, sin lies at the door. And to you shall be his desire, and you shall rule over him.

(Jasher 1:17)

And in some time after, Cain and Abel his brother, went one day into the field to do their work; and they were both in the field, Cain tilling and ploughing his ground, and Abel feeding his flock; and the flock passed that part which Cain had ploughed in the ground, and it sorely grieved Cain on this account.

(Jasher 1:18)

And Cain approached his brother Abel in anger, and he said to him, What is there between me and you, that you come to dwell and bring your flock to feed in my land?

(Jasher 1:19)

And Abel answered his brother Cain and said to him, What is there between me and you, that you shall eat the flesh of my flock and clothe yourself with their wool?

(Jasher 1:20)
And now therefore, put off the wool of my sheep with which you have clothed yourself, and recompense me for their fruit and flesh which you have eaten, and when you shall have done this, I will then go from your land as you have said?

(Genesis 4:8...)

And Cain talked with Abel his brother: and it came to pass, when they were in the field...

(Jasher 1:21)
Cain said to his brother Abel, Surely if I slay you this day, who will require your blood from me?

(Jasher 1:22)
And Abel answered Cain, saying, Surely God who has made us in the earth, He will avenge my cause, and He will require my blood from you should you slay me, for the Lord is the judge and arbiter, and it is He who will requite man according to his evil, and the wicked man according to the wickedness that he may do on earth.

(Jasher 1:23)
And now, if you should slay me here, surely God knows your secret views, and will judge you for the evil which you declare to do to me this day.

(Jasher 1:24)
And when Cain heard the words which Abel his brother had spoken, behold the anger of Cain was kindled against his brother Abel for declaring this thing.

(...Genesis 4:8) (Jasher 1:25...)

And Cain hastened and Cain rose up against Abel his brother, and took the iron part of his ploughing instrument, with which he suddenly slew him.

(Jubilees 4:2)
And in the first year of the third jubilee, Cain slew Abel because God accepted the sacrifice of Abel, and did not accept the offering of Cain.

(...Jasher 1:25)
And Cain spilled the blood of his brother Abel on the earth, and the blood of Abel streamed on the earth before the flock.

(Jubilees 4:3)
And he slew him in the field: and his blood cried from the ground to heaven, complaining because he had slain him.

(Jasher 1:26)
And after this Cain repented having slain his brother, and he was sadly grieved, and he wept over him and it vexed him exceedingly.

(Jasher 1:27)
And Cain rose up and dug a hole in the field, wherein he put his brother's body, and he turned the dust over it.

(Jasher 1:28...)
And the Lord knew what Cain had done to his brother, and the Lord appeared to Cain...

(Genesis 4:9) (...Jasher 1:28, 29)
And the Lord said to Cain, Where is Abel your brother that was with you? And Cain dissembled and said, I do not know: Am I my brother's keeper?

(Genesis 4:10) (...Jasher 1:29)
And the Lord said, What have you done? The voice of your brother's blood cries to Me from the ground where you have slain him.

(Jasher 1:30)
For you have slain your brother and have dissembled before Me, and imagined in your heart that I did not see you, nor knew all your actions.

(Jasher 1:31...)
But you did this thing and slayed your brother for naught and because he spoke rightly to you.

~ ~ ~

(Enoch 22:1)
From there I proceeded to another spot, where I saw on the west a great and lofty mountain, a strong rock, and four delightful places.

(Enoch 22:2)
Internally it was deep, capacious, and very smooth; as smooth as if it had been rolled over: it was both deep and dark to behold.

(Enoch 22:3)
Then Raphael, one of the holy angels who was with me, answered and said, These are the delightful places where the spirits, the souls of the dead, will be collected; for them were they formed; and here will be collected all the souls of the sons of men.

(Enoch 22:4)
These places, in which they dwell, shall they occupy until the day of judgment, and until their appointed period.

(Enoch 22:5)
Their appointed period will be long, even until the great judgment. And I saw the spirits of the sons of men who were dead; and their voices reached to heaven, while they were accusing.

(Enoch 22:6)
Then I inquired of Raphael, an angel who was with me, and said, Whose spirit is that, the voice of which reaches to heaven, and accuses?

(Enoch 22:7)
He answered, saying, This is the spirit of Abel, who was slain by Cain his brother; and who will accuse that brother, until his seed is destroyed from the face of the earth;

(Enoch 22:8)
Until his seed perish from the seed of the human race.

(Enoch 22:9)
At that time therefore I inquired respecting him, and respecting the general judgment, saying, Why is one separated from another? He answered, Three separations have been made between the spirits of the dead, and thus have the spirits of the righteous been separated.

(Enoch 22:10)
Namely, by a chasm, by water, and by light above it.

(Enoch 22:11)
And in the same way likewise are sinners separated when they die, and are buried in the earth; judgment not overtaking them in their lifetime.

(Enoch 22:12)
Here their souls are separated. Moreover, abundant is their suffering until the time of the great judgment, the castigation, and the torment of those who eternally execrate, whose souls are punished and bound there forever.

(Enoch 22:13)
And thus, has it been from the beginning of the world. Thus has there existed a separation between the souls of those who utter complaints, and of those who watch for their destruction, to slaughter them in the day of sinners.

(Enoch 22:14)
A receptacle of this sort has been formed for the souls of unrighteous men, and of sinners; of those who have completed crime, and associated with the impious, whom they resemble. Their souls shall not be annihilated in the day of judgment, neither shall they arise from this place. Then I blessed God,

(Enoch 22:15)
And said, Blessed be my Lord, the Lord of glory and of righteousness, who reigns over all forever and forever.

~ ~ ~

(Genesis 4:11) (...Jasher 1:31)

And now therefore, you are cursed from the earth, which has opened her mouth to receive your brother's blood from your hand; and wherein you buried him.

(Genesis 4:12) (Jasher 1:32)

And it shall be when you till the ground, it shall not from here on out yield to you her strength as in the beginning, for thorns and thistles shall the ground produce; a fugitive and a vagabond shall you be in the earth. And you shall be moving and wandering in the earth until the day of your death.

(Jubilees 4:4)

And the Lord reproved Cain because of Abel, because he had slain him, and he made him a fugitive on the earth because of the blood of his brother, and he cursed him on the earth.

(Jubilees 4:5)

And on this account, it is written on the heavenly tables, Cursed is he who smites his neighbor treacherously, and let all who have seen and heard say, So be it; and the man who has seen and not declared it, let him be accursed as the other.

(Jubilees 4:6)

And for this reason, we announce when we come before the Lord our God all the sin which is committed in heaven and on earth, and in light and in darkness, and everywhere.

(Genesis 4:13)

And Cain said to the Lord, My punishment is greater than I can bear.

(Genesis 4:14)

Behold, you have driven me out this day from the face of

the earth; and from your face I shall be hid; and I shall be a fugitive and a vagabond in the earth; and it shall come to pass, that everyone that finds me shall slay me.

(Genesis 4:15)

And the Lord said to him, Therefore, whosoever slays Cain, vengeance shall be taken on him sevenfold. And the Lord set a mark on Cain, lest any finding him should kill him.

(Genesis 4:16) (Jasher 1:33)

And at that time Cain went out from the presence of the Lord, from the place where he was, and he went moving and wandering in the land toward the east of Eden, he and all belonging to him; and dwelt in the land of Nod, on the east of Eden.

(Genesis 4:17...) (Jasher 1:34) (Jubilees 4:9...)

And Cain took Âwân his sister to be his wife. And Cain knew his wife in those days, and she conceived, and bore him a son, and he called his name Enoch at the close of the fourth jubilee, saying, In that time, the Lord began to give him rest and quiet in the earth.

(...Genesis 4:17) (Jasher 1:35) (...Jubilees 4:9)

And in the first year of the first week of the fifth jubilee, houses were built on the earth, and at that time Cain also began to build a city, and called the name of the city, after the name of his son, Enoch, for in those days the Lord had given him rest on the earth, and he did not move about and wander as in the beginning.

(Genesis 4:18) (Jasher 1:36)

And to Enoch was born Irad: and Irad begot Mehujael: and Mehujael begot Methusael: and Methusael begot Lamech.

(Genesis 4:19) (Jasher 2:17...)
And Lamech took to him two wives: the name of the one was Adah, and the name of the other Zillah.

(Genesis 4:20) (...Jasher 2:17...)
And Adah conceived and bore a son to Lamech, and she called his name Jabal: he was the father of such as dwell in tents, and of such as have cattle.

(Genesis 4:21) (Jasher 2:18)
And she again conceived and bore a son, his brother, and called his name Jubal: he was the father of all such as handle the harp and organ. And Zillah, her sister, was barren in those days and had no offspring.

~ ~ ~

(Jasher 2:19)
For in those days the sons of men began to trespass against God, and to transgress the commandments which he had commanded to Adam, to be fruitful and multiply in the earth.

(Jasher 2:20)
And some of the sons of men caused their wives to drink a draught that would render them barren, in order that they might retain their figures and whereby their beautiful appearance might not fade.

(Jasher 2:21)
And when the sons of men caused some of their wives to drink, Zillah drank with them.

(Jasher 2:22)
And the child-bearing women appeared abominable in the sight of their husbands as widows, while their husbands lived, for to the barren ones only they were attached.

(Jasher 2:23)
And in the end of days and years, when Zillah became old, the Lord opened her womb.

(Genesis 4:22...) (Jasher 2:24)
And Zillah, she conceived and bore a son and she called his name Tubal Cain, saying, After I had withered away have I obtained him from the Almighty God.

(...Genesis 4:22) (Jasher 2:25)
Tubal Cain was an instructor of every artificer in brass and iron. And she conceived again and bore a daughter, the sister of Tubal Cain and she called her name Naamah, for she said, After I had withered away have I obtained pleasure and delight.

(Jasher 2:26)
And Lamech was old and advanced in years, and his eyes were dim that he could not see, and Tubal Cain, his son, was leading him and it was one day that Lamech went into the field and Tubal Cain his son was with him, and while they were walking in the field, Cain the son of Adam advanced towards them; for Lamech was very old and could not see much, and Tubal Cain his son was very young.

(Jasher 2:27)
And Tubal Cain told his father to draw his bow, and with the arrows he smote Cain, who was yet far off, and he slew him, for he appeared to them to be an animal.

(Jasher 2:28)
And the arrows entered Cain's body although he was distant from them, and he fell to the ground and died.

(Jasher 2:29)
And the Lord requited Cain's evil according to his wickedness, which he was done to his brother Abel, according to the word of the Lord which he had spoken.

(Jasher 2:30)
And it came to pass when Cain had died, that Lamech and Tubal went to see the animal which they had slain, and they saw, and behold Cain their grandfather was fallen dead on the earth.

(Jasher 2:31)
And Lamech was very much grieved at having done this, and in clapping his hands together he struck his son and caused his death.

(Jasher 2:32)
And the wives of Lamech heard what Lamech was done, and they sought to kill him.

(Jasher 2:33)
And the wives of Lamech hated him from that day, because he slew Cain and Tubal Cain, and the wives of Lamech separated from him, and would not hearken to him in those days.

(Jasher 2:34)
And Lamech came to his wives, and he pressed them to listen to him about this matter.

(Genesis 4:23) (Jasher 2:35...)

And Lamech said to his wives, Adah and Zillah, Hear my voice; you wives of Lamech, hearken to my speech, attend to my words: for I have slain a man to my wounding, and a young man to my hurt.

(...Jasher 2:35)

For now you have imagined and said that I slew a man with my wounds, and a child with my stripes for their having done no violence, but surely know that I am old and gray-headed, and that my eyes are heavy through age, and I did this thing unknowingly.

(Jasher 2:36)

And the wives of Lamech listened to him in this matter, and they returned to him with the advice of their father Adam, but they bore no children to him from that time, knowing that God's anger was increasing in those days against the sons of men, to destroy them with the waters of the flood for their evil doings.

(Genesis 4:24)

If Cain shall be avenged sevenfold, truly Lamech seventy and sevenfold.

~ ~ ~

(Jubilees 4:31)

At the close of the nineteenth jubilee Cain was killed after him in the same year; for his house fell on him and he died in the midst of his house, and he was killed by its stones; for with a stone he had killed Abel, and by a stone was he killed in righteous judgment.

(Jubilees 4:32)
For this reason it was ordained on the heavenly tablets: With the instrument with which a man kills his neighbor with the same shall he be killed; after the manner that he wounded him, in like manner shall they deal with him.

~ ~ ~

(Genesis 4:25) (Jasher 2:1) (Jubilees 4:7)
And Adam and his wife mourned for Abel four weeks of years, and in the fourth year of the fifth week, they became joyful, and Adam knew his wife again; and she conceived and bore a son, and called his name Seth: saying For God has appointed me another seed instead of Abel, whom Cain slew.

(Jubilees 4:8)
And in the sixth week, he begot his daughter Azûrâ.

(Genesis 4:26)
And to Seth, to him also there was born a son; and he called his name Enosh: then began men to call on the name of the Lord.

Genesis: Chapter Five

(Genesis 5:1)
This is the book of the generations of Adam. In the day that God created man, in the likeness of God made he him;

(Genesis 5:2) (...Jasher 1:6)
Male and female, He created them; and God blessed them, and called their names Adam and Eve, in the day when they were created.

(Genesis 5:3) (...Jasher 2:1)
And Adam lived a hundred and thirty years on the earth and begot a son in his own likeness, after his image; and she called his name Seth:

(Genesis 5:4) (Jubilees 4:10)
And the days of Adam after he had begotten Seth were eight hundred years: And Adam knew Eve his wife and he begot sons and daughters - she bore yet nine sons and daughters:

(Jubilees 4:29)
And at the close of the nineteenth jubilee, in the seventh week in the sixth year thereof, Adam died, and all his sons buried him in the land of his creation, and he was the first to be buried in the earth.

(Jubilees 4:30)
And he lacked seventy years of one thousand years; for one thousand years are as one day in the testimony of the heavens and therefore was it written concerning the tree of knowledge:

On the day that you eat thereof you shall die. For this reason, he did not complete the years of this day; for he died during it.

(Genesis 5:5)

And all the days that Adam lived were nine hundred and thirty years: and he died.

(Jubilees 4:11)

And in the fifth week of the fifth jubilee, Seth took Azûrâ his sister to be his wife,

(Genesis 5:6) (Jasher 2:2) (Jubilees 4:11)

And Seth lived a hundred and five years, and in the fourth (year of the sixth week) begot a son; she bore him and Seth called the name of his son Enosh: saying, Because in that time the sons of men began to multiply, and to afflict their souls and hearts by transgressing and rebelling against God.

(Jubilees 4:12)

He began to call on the name of the Lord on the earth.

(Jasher 2:3)

And it was in the days of Enosh that the sons of men continued to rebel and transgress against God, to increase the anger of the Lord against the sons of men.

(Jasher 2:4)

And the sons of men went and they served other gods, and they forgot the Lord who had created them in the earth: and in those days the sons of men made images of brass and iron, wood and stone, and they bowed down and served them.

(Jasher 2:5)

And every man made his God and they bowed down to them,

and the sons of men forsook the Lord all the days of Enosh and his children; and the anger of the Lord was kindled on account of their works and abominations which they did in the earth.

(Jasher 2:6)
And the Lord caused the waters of the river Gihon to overwhelm them, and he destroyed and consumed them, and he destroyed the third part of the earth, and notwithstanding this, the sons of men did not turn from their evil ways, and their hands were yet extended to do evil in the sight of the Lord.

(Jasher 2:7)
And in those days, there was neither sowing nor reaping in the earth; and there was no food for the sons of men and the famine was very great in those days.

(Jasher 2:8)
And the seed which they sowed in those days in the ground became thorns, thistles and briers; for from the days of Adam was this declaration concerning the earth, of the curse of God, which he cursed the earth, on account of the sin which Adam sinned before the Lord.

(Jasher 2:9)
And it was when men continued to rebel and transgress against God, and to corrupt their ways, that the earth also became corrupt.

(Genesis 5:7)
And Seth lived after he begot Enosh eight hundred and seven years, and begot sons and daughters:

(Genesis 5:8) (Jasher 4:10)

And all the days of Seth were nine hundred and twelve years: and he died.

(Genesis 5:9) (Jasher 2:10) (Jubilees 4:13)

And Enosh lived ninety years. And in the seventh jubilee in the third week, Enosh took Nôâm his sister to be his wife, and she bore him a son in the third year of the fifth week and he called his name Cainan.

(Genesis 5:10)

And Enosh lived after he begot Cainan eight hundred and fifteen years, and begot sons and daughters:

(Genesis 5:11) (Jasher 5:1)

And all the days of Enosh were nine hundred and five years at his death: And it was in the eighty-fourth year of the life of Noah, that Enoch the son of Seth died.

(Jasher 2:11)

And Cainan grew up and he was forty years old, and he became wise and had knowledge and skill in all wisdom, and he reigned over all the sons of men, and he led the sons of men to wisdom and knowledge; for Cainan was a very wise man and had understanding in all wisdom, and with his wisdom he ruled over spirits and demons;

(Jasher 2:12)

And Cainan knew by his wisdom that God would destroy the sons of men for having sinned on earth, and that the Lord would in the latter days bring on them the waters of the flood.

(Jasher 2:13)

And in those days Cainan wrote on tablets of stone, what was to take place in time to come, and he put them in his treasures.

(Jasher 2:14)
And Cainan reigned over the whole earth, and he turned some of the sons of men to the service of God.

(Jubilees 4:14...)
And at the close of the eighth jubilee, Kenan took Mûalêlêth his sister to be his wife, and she bore him a son in the ninth jubilee, in the first week in the third year of this week.

(Genesis 5:12...) (Jasher 2:15)

And Cainan lived seventy years, and begot three sons and two daughters;

(...Genesis 5:12) (Jasher 2:16) (...Jubilees 4:14)

And these are the names of the children of Cainan; and he called the name of the first born Mahalaleel, the second Enan, and the third Mered, and their sisters were Adah and Zillah; these are the five children of Cainan that were born to him.

(Jasher 2:17)
And Lamech, the son of Methusael, became related to Cainan by marriage, and he took his two daughters for his wives...

(Genesis 5:13)

And Cainan lived after he begot Mahalaleel eight hundred and forty years, and begot sons and daughters:

(Genesis 5:14) (Jasher 5:2)

And in the one hundred and seventy ninth year of the life of Noah, Cainan the son of Enosh died, and all the days of Cainan were nine hundred and ten years: and he died.

(Jubilees 4:15...)
And in the second week of the tenth jubilee, Mahalalel took to him to wife Dinah, the daughter of Barakiel the daughter of his father's brother.

(Genesis 5:15) (Jasher 2:37...) (...Jubilees 4:15)
And Mahalaleel the son of Cainan lived sixty and five years, and begot a son in the third week in the sixth year, and he called his name Jared: for in his days the angels of the Lord descended on the earth, those who are named the Watchers, that they should instruct the children of men, and that they should do judgment and uprightness on the earth.

(Genesis 5:16)
And Mahalaleel lived after he begot Jared eight hundred and thirty years, and begot sons and daughters:

(Genesis 5:17) (Jasher 5:3)
And in the two hundred and thirty fourth year of the life of Noah, Mahlallel the son of Cainan died, and all the days of Mahalaleel were eight hundred and ninety-five years: and he died.

(Jubilees 4:16)
And in the eleventh jubilee, Jared took to himself a wife, and her name was Baraka, the daughter of Râsûjâl, a daughter of his father's brother, in the fourth week of this jubilee.

(Genesis 5:18) (...Jasher 2:37) (Jubilees 4:16)
And Jared lived a hundred sixty-two years, and he begot a son in the fifth week, in the fourth year of the jubilee, and he called his name Enoch:

(Jubilees 4:17)
And he was the first among men that are born on earth who learned writing and knowledge and wisdom and who wrote down the signs of heaven according to the order of their months in a book, that men might know the seasons of the years according to the order of their separate months.

(Jubilees 4:18)
And he was the first to write a testimony and he testified to the sons of men among the generations of the earth, and recounted the weeks of the jubilees, and made known to them the days of the years, and set in order the months and recounted the Sabbaths of the years as we made known to him.

(Jubilees 4:19)
And what was and what will be he saw in a vision of his sleep, as it will happen to the children of men throughout their generations until the day of judgment; he saw and understood everything, and wrote his testimony, and placed the testimony on earth for all the children of men and for their generations.

(Genesis 5:19)

And Jared lived after he begot Enoch eight hundred years, and begot sons and daughters:

(Genesis 5:20) (Jasher 5:4)

And Jared the son of Mahlallel died in those days, in the three hundred and thirty-sixth year of the life of Noah; and all the days of Jared were nine hundred sixty-two years: and he died.

(Jubilees 4:20...)
And in the twelfth jubilee, in the seventh week thereof, Enoch took to himself a wife, and her name was Edna, the daughter of Danel, the daughter of his father's brother.

(Genesis 5:21) (Jasher 3:1...) (...Jubilees 4:20)
And Enoch lived sixty-five years, and in the sixth year in this week and begot a son and he called his name Methuselah:

(Enoch 81:1)
Now, my son Mathusala, all these things I speak to you, and write for you. To you I have revealed all, and have given you books of everything.

(Enoch 81:2)
Preserve, my son Mathusala, the books written by your father; that you may transmit them to future generations.

(Enoch 81:3)
Wisdom have I given to you, to your children, and your posterity, that they may transmit to their children, for generations forever, this wisdom in their thoughts; and that those who comprehend it may not slumber, but hear with their ears; that they may learn this wisdom, and be deemed worthy of eating this wholesome food.

(Enoch 81:4)
Blessed are all the righteous; blessed all who walk in the paths of righteousness; in whom no crime is found, as in sinners, when all their days are numbered.

~ ~ ~

(Enoch 82:1)
And now I have shown you, my son Mathusala, every sight which I saw prior to your birth. I will relate another vision,

which I saw before I was married; they resemble each other.

(Enoch 82:2)
The first was when I was learning a book; and the other before I was married to your mother. I saw a potent vision;

(Enoch 82:3)
And on account of these things, I besought the Lord.

(Enoch 82:4)
I was lying down in the house of my grandfather Malalel, when I saw in a vision heaven purifying, and snatched away.

(Enoch 82:5)
And falling to the earth, I saw likewise the earth absorbed by a great abyss; and mountains suspended over mountains.

(Enoch 82:6)
Hills were sinking upon hills, lofty trees were gliding off from their trunks, and were in the act of being projected, and of sinking into the abyss.

(Enoch 82:7)
Being alarmed at these things, my voice faltered. I cried out and said,The earth is destroyed. Then my grandfather Malalel raised me up, and said to me: Why do you thus cry out, my son? And why do you thus lament?

(Enoch 82:8)
I related to him the whole vision which I had seen. He said to me, Confirmed is that which you have seen, my son;

(Enoch 82:9)
And potent the vision of your dream respecting every secret

sin of the earth. Its substance shall sink into the abyss, and a great destruction take place.

(Enoch 82:10)
Now, my son, rise up; and beseech the Lord of glory (for you are faithful), that a remnant may be left upon earth, and that he would not wholly destroy it. My son, all this calamity upon earth comes down from heaven; upon earth shall there be a great destruction.

(Enoch 82:11)
Then I arose, prayed, and entreated; and wrote down my prayer for the generations of the world, explaining everything to my son Mathusala.

(Enoch 82:12)
When I went out below, and looking up to heaven, beheld the sun proceeding from the east, the moon descending to the west, a few scattered stars, and everything which God has known from the beginning, I blessed the Lord of judgment, and magnified him: because he hath sent forth the sun from the chambers of the east; that, ascending and rising in the face of heaven, it might spring up, and pursue the path which has been pointed out to it.

~ ~ ~

(Enoch 83:1)
I lifted up my hands in righteousness, and blessed the holy, and the great one. I spoke with the breath of my mouth, and with a tongue of flesh, which God has formed for all the sons of mortal men, that with it they may speak; giving them breath,

a mouth, and a tongue to converse with.

(Enoch 83:2)
Blessed are you, O Lord, the king, great and powerful in your greatness, Lord of all the creatures of heaven, king of kings, God of the whole world, whose reign, whose kingdom, and whose majesty endure forever and ever.

(Enoch 83:3)
From generation to generation shall your dominion exist. All the heavens are your throne forever, and all the earth your footstool forever and forever.

(Enoch 83:4)
For you have made them, and over all you reign. No act whatsoever exceeds your power. With you wisdom is unchangeable; nor from your throne and from your presence is it ever averted. You know all things, see and hear them; nor is anything concealed from you; for you perceive all things.

(Enoch 83:5)
The angels of your heavens have transgressed; and on mortal flesh shall your wrath remain, until the day of the great judgment.

(Enoch 83:6)
Now then, O God, Lord and mighty king, I entreat you, and beseech you to grant my prayer, that a posterity may be left to me on earth, and that the whole human race may not perish;

(Enoch 83:7)
That the earth may not be left destitute, and destruction take place forever.

(Enoch 83:8)
O my Lord, let the race perish from off the earth which has offended you, but a righteous and upright race establish for a posterity forever. Hide not your face, O Lord, from the prayer of your servant.

~ ~ ~

(Enoch 84:1)
After this I saw another dream, and explained it all to you, my son. Enoch arose and said to his son Mathusala, To you, my son, will I speak. Hear my word; and incline your ear to the visionary dream of your father. Before I married your mother Edna, I saw a vision on my bed;

(Enoch 84:2)
And behold, a cow sprung forth from the earth;

(Enoch 84:3)
And this cow was white.

(Enoch 84:4)
Afterwards a female heifer sprung forth; and with it another heifer: one of them was black, and one was red.

(Enoch 84:5)
The black heifer then struck the red one, and pursued it over the earth.

(Enoch 84:6)
From that period, I could see nothing more of the red heifer;

but the black one increased in bulk, and a female heifer came with him.

(Enoch 84:7)
After this I saw that many cows proceeded forth, resembling him, and following after him.

(Enoch 84:8)
The first female young one also went out in the presence of the first cow; and sought the red heifer; but found him not.

(Enoch 84:9)
And she lamented with a great lamentation, while she was seeking him.

(Enoch 84:10)
Then I looked until that first cow came to her, from which time she became silent, and ceased to lament.

(Enoch 84:11)
Afterwards she calved another white cow.

(Enoch 84:12)
And again calved many cows and black heifers.

(Enoch 84:13)
In my sleep, I also perceived a white bull, which in like manner grew, and became a large white bull.

(Enoch 84:14)
After him many white cows came forth, resembling him.

(Enoch 84:15)
And they began to calve many other white cows, which resembled them and followed each other.

~ ~ ~

(Enoch 85:1)
Again, I looked attentively, while sleeping, and surveyed heaven above.

(Enoch 85:2)
And behold a single star fell from heaven.

(Enoch 85:3)
Which being raised up, ate and fed among those cows.

(Enoch 85:4)
After that I perceived other large and black cows; and behold all of them changed their stalls and pastures, while their young began to lament one with another. Again, I looked in my vision, and surveyed heaven; when behold I saw many stars which descended, and projected themselves from heaven to where the first star was,

(Enoch 85:5)
Into the midst of those young ones; while the cows were with them, feeding in the midst of them.

(Enoch 85:61)
I looked at and observed them; when behold, they all acted after the manner of horses, and began to approach the young

cows, all of whom became pregnant, and brought forth elephants, camels, and donkeys.

(Enoch 85:7)
At these all the cows were alarmed and terrified; when they began biting with their teeth, swallowing, and striking with their horns.

(Enoch 85:8)
They began also to devour the cows; and behold all the children of the earth trembled, shook with terror at them, and suddenly fled away.

~ ~ ~

(Enoch 86:1)
Again, I perceived them, when they began to strike and to swallow each other; and the earth cried out. Then I raised my eyes a second time towards heaven, and saw in a vision, that, behold, there came forth from heaven as it were the likeness of white men. One came forth from there, and three with him.

(Enoch 86:2)
Those three, who came forth last, seized me by my hand; and raising me up from the generations of the earth, elevated me to a high station.

(Enoch 86:3)
Then they showed me a lofty tower on the earth, while every hill became diminished. And they said, Remain here, until you perceive what shall come upon those elephants, camels, and donkeys, upon the stars, and upon all the cows.

~ ~ ~

(Enoch 87:1)
Then I looked at that one of the four white men, who came forth first.

(Enoch 87:2)
He seized the first star which fell down from heaven.

(Enoch 87:3)
And, binding it hand and foot, he cast it into a valley; a valley narrow, deep, stupendous, and gloomy.

(Enoch 87:4)
Then one of them drew his sword, and gave it to the elephants, camels, and donkeys, who began to strike each other. And the whole earth shook on account of them.

(Enoch 87:5)
And when I looked in the vision, behold, one of those four angels, who came forth, hurled from heaven, collected together, and took all the great stars, whose form partly resembled that of horses; and binding them all hand and foot, cast them into the cavities of the earth.

~ ~ ~

(Enoch 88:1)
Then one of those four went to the white cows, and taught them a mystery. While the cow was trembling, it was born,

and became a man, and fabricated for himself a large ship. In this he dwelt, and three cows dwelt with him in that ship, which covered them.

(Enoch 88:2)
Again, I lifted up my eyes towards heaven, and saw a lofty roof. Above it were seven cataracts, which poured forth on a certain village much water.

(Enoch 88:3)
Again, I looked, and behold there were fountains open on the earth in that large village.

(Enoch 88:4)
The water began to boil up, and rose over the earth; so that the village was not seen, while its whole soil was covered with water.

(Enoch 88:5)
Much water was over it, darkness, and clouds. Then I surveyed the height of this water; and it was elevated above the village.

(Enoch 88:6)
It flowed over the village, and stood higher than the earth.

(Enoch 88:7)
Then all the cows which were collected there, while I looked on them, were drowned, swallowed up, and destroyed in the water.

(Enoch 88:8)
But the ship floated above it. All the cows, the elephants, the camels, and the donkeys, were drowned on the earth, and all cattle. Nor could I perceive them. Neither were they able to

get out, but perished, and sunk into the deep.

(Enoch 88:9)
Again, I looked in the vision until those cataracts from that lofty roof were removed, and the fountains of the earth became equalized, while other depths were opened;

(Enoch 88:10)
Into which the water began to descend, until the dry ground appeared.

(Enoch 88:11)
The ship remained on the earth; the darkness receded; and it became light.

(Enoch 88:12)
Then the white cow, which became a man, went out of the ship, and the three cows with him.

(Enoch 88:13)
One of the three cows was white, resembling that cow; one of them was red as blood; and one of them was black. And the white cow left them.

(Enoch 88:14)
Then began wild beasts and birds to bring forth.

(Enoch 88:15)
Of all these the different kinds assembled together, lions, tigers, wolves, dogs, wild boars, foxes, rabbits, and the hanzar,

(Enoch 88:16)
The siset, the avest, kites, the phonkas, and ravens.

(Enoch 88:17)
Then a white cow was born in the midst of them.

(Enoch 88:18)
And they began to bite each other; when the white cow, which was born in the midst of them, brought forth a wild donkey and a white cow at the same time, and after that many wild donkeys. Then the white cow, which was born, brought forth a black wild sow and a white sheep.

(Enoch 88:19)
That wild sow also brought forth many swine;

(Enoch 88:20)
And that sheep brought forth twelve sheep.

(Enoch 88:21)
When those twelve sheep grew up, they delivered one of them to the donkeys.

(Enoch 88:22)
Again, those donkeys delivered that sheep to the wolves;

(Enoch 88:23)
And he grew up in the midst of them.

(Enoch 88:24)
Then the Lord brought the eleven other sheep, that they might dwell and feed with him in the midst of the wolves.

(Enoch 88:25)
They multiplied, and there was abundance of pasture for them.

(Enoch 88:26)
But the wolves began to frighten and oppress them, while they destroyed their young ones.

(Enoch 88:27)
And they left their young in torrents of deep water.

(Enoch 88:28)
Now the sheep began to cry out on account of their young, and fled for refuge to their Lord. One however, which was saved, escaped, and went away to the wild donkeys.

(Enoch 88:29)
I beheld the sheep moaning, crying, and petitioning their Lord,

(Enoch 88:30)
With all their might, until the Lord of the sheep descended at their voice from his lofty habitation; went to them; and inspected them.

(Enoch 88:31)
He called to that sheep which had secretly stolen away from the wolves, and told him to make the wolves understand that they were not to touch the sheep.

(Enoch 88:32)
Then that sheep went to the wolves with the word of the Lord, when another met him, and proceeded with him.

(Enoch 88:33)
Both of them together entered the dwelling of the wolves; and conversing with them made them understand, that from there on out they were not to touch the sheep.

(Enoch 88:34)
Afterwards I perceived the wolves greatly prevailing over the sheep with their whole force. The sheep cried out; and their Lord came to them.

(Enoch 88:35)
He began to strike the wolves, who commenced a grievous lamentation; but the sheep were silent, nor from that time did they cry out.

(Enoch 88:36)
I then looked at them, until they departed from the wolves. The eyes of the wolves were blind, who went out and followed them with all their might. But the Lord of the sheep proceeded with them, and conducted them.

(Enoch 88:37)
All his sheep followed him.

(Enoch 88:38)
His countenance was terrific and splendid, and glorious was his aspect. Yet the wolves began to follow the sheep, until they overtook them in a certain lake of water.

(Enoch 88:39)
Then that lake became divided; the water standing up on both sides before their face.

(Enoch 88:40)
And while their Lord was conducting them, he placed himself between them and the wolves.

(Enoch 88:41)
The wolves however perceived not the sheep, but went into

the midst of the lake, following them, and running after them into the lake of water.

(Enoch 88:42)
But when they saw the Lord of the sheep, they turned to fly from before his face.

(Enoch 88:43)
Then the water of the lake returned, and that suddenly, according to its nature. It became full, and was raised up, until it covered the wolves. And I saw that all of them which had followed the sheep perished, and were drowned.

(Enoch 88:44)
But the sheep passed over this water, proceeding to a wilderness, which was without both water and grass. And they began to open their eves and to see.

(Enoch 88:45)
Then I beheld the Lord of the sheep inspecting them, and giving them water and grass.

(Enoch 88:46)
The sheep already mentioned was proceeding with them, and conducting them.

(Enoch 88:47)
And when he had ascended the top of a lofty rock, the Lord of the sheep sent him to them.

(Enoch 88:48)
Afterwards I perceived their Lord standing before them, with an aspect terrific and severe.

(Enoch 88:49)
And when they all beheld him, they were frightened at his countenance.

(Enoch 88:50)
All of them were alarmed, and trembled. They cried out after that sheep; and to the other sheep who had been with him, and who was in the midst of them, saying, We are not able to stand before our Lord, or to look upon him.

(Enoch 88:51)
Then that sheep who conducted them went away, and ascended the top of the rock;

(Enoch 88:52)
When the rest of the sheep began to grow blind, and to wander from the path which he had shown them; but he knew it not.

(Enoch 88:53)
Their Lord however was moved with great indignation against them; and when that sheep had learned what had happened,

(Enoch 88:54)
He descended from the top of the rock, and coming to them, found that there were many,

(Enoch 88:55)
Which had become blind;

(Enoch 88:56)
And had wandered from his path. As soon as they beheld him, they feared, and trembled at his presence;

(Enoch 88:57)
And became desirous of returning to their fold.

(Enoch 88:58)
Then that sheep, taking with him other sheep, went to those which had wandered.

(Enoch 88:59)
And afterwards began to kill them. They were terrified at his countenance. Then he caused those which had wandered to return; who went back to their fold.

(Enoch 88:60)
I likewise saw there in the vision, that this sheep became a man, built a house for the Lord of the sheep, and made them all stand in that house.

(Enoch 88:61)
I perceived also that the sheep which proceeded to meet this sheep, their conductor, died. I saw, too, that all the great sheep perished, while smaller ones rose up in their place, entered into a pasture, and approached a river of water.

(Enoch 88:62)
Then that sheep, their conductor, who became a man, was separated from them, and died.

(Enoch 88:63)
All the sheep sought after him, and cried for him with bitter lamentation.

(Enoch 88:64)
I saw likewise that they ceased to cry after that sheep, and passed over the river of water.

(Enoch 88:65)
And that there arose other sheep, all of whom conducted them, instead of those who were dead, and who had previously conducted them.

(Enoch 88:66)
Then I saw that the sheep entered into a goodly place, and a territory delectable and glorious.

(Enoch 88:67)
I saw also that they became satiated; that their house was in the midst of a delectable territory: and that sometimes their eyes were opened, and that sometimes they were blind; until another sheep arose and conducted them. He brought them all back; and their eyes were opened.

(Enoch 88:68)
Then dogs, foxes, and wild boars began to devour them, until again another sheep arose, the master of the flock, one of themselves, a ram, to conduct them. This ram began to butt on every side those dogs, foxes, and wild boars, until they all perished.

(Enoch 88:69)
But the former sheep opened his eyes, and saw the ram in the midst of them, who had laid aside his glory.

(Enoch 88:70)
And he began to strike the sheep, treading upon them, and behaving himself without dignity.

(Enoch 88:71)
Then their Lord sent the former sheep again to a still different sheep, and raised him up to be a ram, and to conduct them

instead of that sheep who had laid aside his glory.

(Enoch 88:72)
Going therefore to him, and conversing with him alone, he raised up that ram, and made him a prince and leader of the flock. All the time that the dogs troubled the sheep,

(Enoch 88:73)
The first ram paid respect to this latter ram.

(Enoch 88:74)
Then the latter ram arose, and fled away from before his face. And I saw that those dogs caused the first ram to fall.

(Enoch 88:75)
But the latter ram arose, and conducted the smaller sheep.

(Enoch 88:76)
That ram likewise begot many sheep, and died.

(Enoch 88:77)
Then there was a smaller sheep, a ram, instead of him, which became a prince and leader, conducting the flock.

(Enoch 88:78)
And the sheep increased in size, and multiplied.

(Enoch 88:79)
And all the dogs, foxes, and wild boars feared, and fled away from him.

(Enoch 88:80)
That ram also struck and killed all the wild beasts, so that

they could not again prevail in the midst of the sheep, nor at any time ever snatch them away.

(Enoch 88:81)
And that house was made large and wide; a lofty tower being built upon it by the sheep, for the Lord of the sheep.

(Enoch 88:82)
The house was low, but the tower was elevated and very high.

(Enoch 88:83)
Then the Lord of the sheep stood upon that tower, and caused a full table to approach before him.

(Enoch 88:84)
Again, I saw that those sheep wandered, and went various ways, forsaking that their house;

(Enoch 88:85)
And that their Lord called to some among them, whom he sent to them.

(Enoch 88:86)
But these the sheep began to kill. And when one of them was saved from slaughter, he leaped, and cried out against those who were desirous of killing him.

(Enoch 88:87)
But the Lord of the sheep delivered him from their hands, and made him ascend to him, and remain with him.

(Enoch 88:88)
He sent also many others to them, to testify, and with lamentations to exclaim against them.

(Enoch 88:89)
Again, I saw, when some of them forsook the house of their Lord, and his tower; wandering on all sides, and growing blind,

(Enoch 88:90)
I saw that the Lord of the sheep made a great slaughter among them in their pasture, until they cried out to him in consequence of that slaughter. Then he departed from the place of his habitation, and left them in the power of lions, tigers, wolves, and the zeebt, and in the power of foxes, and of every beast.

(Enoch 88:91)
And the wild beasts began to tear them.

(Enoch 88:92)
I saw, too, that he forsook the house of their fathers, and their tower; giving them all into the power of lions to tear and devour them; into the power of every beast.

(Enoch 88:93)
Then I began to cry out with all my might, imploring the Lord of the sheep, and showing him how the sheep were devoured by all the beasts of prey.

(Enoch 88:94)
But he looked on in silence, rejoicing that they were devoured, swallowed up, and carried off; and leaving them in the power of every beast for food. He called also seventy shepherds, and resigned to them the care of the sheep, that they might overlook them;

(Enoch 88:95)
Saying to them and to their associates, Every one of you from here on out overlook the sheep, and whatsoever I command you, do; and I will deliver them to you numbered.

(Enoch 88:96)
I will tell you which of them shall be slain; these destroy. And he delivered the sheep to them.

(Enoch 88:97)
Then he called to another, and said, Understand, and watch everything which the shepherds shall do to these sheep; for many more of them shall perish than I have commanded.

(Enoch 88:98)
Of every excess and slaughter, which the shepherds shall commit, there shall be an account; as, how many may have perished by my command, and how many they may have destroyed of their own heads.

(Enoch 88:99)
Of all the destruction brought about by each of the shepherds there shall be an account; and according to the number I will cause a recital to be made before me, how many they have destroyed of their own heads, and how many they have delivered up to destruction, that I may have this testimony against them; that I may know all their proceedings; and that, delivering the sheep to them, I may see what they will do; whether they will act as I have commanded them, or not.

(Enoch 88:100)
Of this, however, they shall be ignorant; neither shall you make any explanation to them, neither shall you reprove them; but there shall be an account of all the destruction done

by them in their respective seasons. Then they began to kill, and destroy more than it was commanded them.

(Enoch 88:101)
And they left the sheep in the power of lions, so that very many of them were devoured and swallowed up by lions and tigers; and wild boars preyed upon them. That tower they burnt, and overthrew that house.

(Enoch 88:102)
Then I grieved extremely on account of the tower, and because the house of the sheep was overthrown.

(Enoch 88:103)
Neither was I afterwards able to perceive whether they again entered that house.

(Enoch 88:104)
The shepherds likewise, and their associates, delivered them to all the wild beasts, that they might devour them. Each of them in his season, according to his number, was delivered up; each of them, one with another, was described in a book, how many of them, one with another, were destroyed, in a book.

(Enoch 88:105)
More, however, than was ordered, every shepherd killed and destroyed.

(Enoch 88:106)
Then I began to weep, and was greatly indignant, on account of the sheep.

(Enoch 88:107)
In like manner, I also saw in the vision him who wrote, how he wrote down one, destroyed by the shepherds, every day. He ascended, remained, and exhibited each of his books to the Lord of the sheep, containing all which they had done, and all which each of them had made away with;

(Enoch 88:108)
And all which they had delivered up to destruction.

(Enoch 88:109)
He took the book up in his hands, read it, sealed it, and deposited it.

(Enoch 88:110)
After this, I saw shepherds overlooking for twelve hours.

(Enoch 88:111)
And behold three of the sheep departed, arrived, went in; and began building all which was fallen down of that house.

(Enoch 88:112)
But the wild boars hindered them, although they prevailed not.

(Enoch 88:113)
Again, they began to build as before, and raised up that tower, which was called a lofty tower.

(Enoch 88:114)
And again, they began to place before the tower a table, with every impure and unclean kind of bread upon it.

(Enoch 88:115)
Moreover, also all the sheep were blind, and could not see; as were the shepherds likewise.

(Enoch 88:116)
Thus, they were delivered up to the shepherds for a great destruction, who trod them under foot, and devoured them.

(Enoch 88:117)
Yet was their Lord silent, until all the sheep in the field were destroyed. The shepherds and the sheep were all mixed together; but they did not save them from the power of the beasts.

(Enoch 88:118)
Then he who wrote the book ascended, exhibited it, and read it at the residence of the Lord of the sheep. He petitioned him for them, and prayed, pointing out every act of the shepherds, and testifying before him against them all. Then taking the book, he deposited it with him, and departed.

~ ~ ~

(Enoch 89:1)
And I observed during the time, that thus thirty-seven shepherds were overlooking, all of whom finished in their respective periods as the first. Others then received them into their hands, that they might overlook them in their respective periods, every shepherd in his own period.

(Enoch 89:2)
Afterwards I saw in the vision, that all the birds of heaven

arrived; eagles, the avest, kites and ravens. The eagle instructed them all.

(Enoch 89:3)
They began to devour the sheep, to peck out their eyes, and to eat up their bodies.

(Enoch 89:4)
The sheep then cried out; for their bodies were devoured by the birds.

(Enoch 89:5)
I also cried out, and groaned in my sleep against that shepherd which overlooked the flock.

(Enoch 89:6)
And I looked, while the sheep were eaten up by the dogs, by the eagles, and by the kites. They neither left them their body, nor their skin, nor their muscles, until their bones alone remained; until their bones fell upon the ground. And the sheep became diminished.

(Enoch 89:7)
I observed likewise during the time, that twenty-three shepherds were overlooking; who completed in their respective periods fifty-eight periods.

(Enoch 89:8)
Then were small lambs born of those white sheep; who began to open their eyes and to see, crying out to the sheep.

(Enoch 89:9)
The sheep, however, cried not out to them, neither did they hear what they uttered to them; but were deaf, blind, and

obdurate in the greatest degrees.

(Enoch 89:10)
I saw in the vision that ravens flew down upon those lambs;

(Enoch 89:11)
That they seized one of them; and that tearing the sheep in pieces, they devoured them.

(Enoch 89:12)
I saw also, that horns grew upon those lambs; and that the ravens lighted down upon their horns.

(Enoch 89:13)
I saw, too, that a large horn sprouted out on an animal among the sheep, and that their eyes were opened.

(Enoch 89:14)
He looked at them. Their eyes were wide open; and he cried out to them.

(Enoch 89:15)
Then the dabela saw him; all of whom ran to him.

(Enoch 89:16)
And besides this, all the eagles, the avest, the ravens and the kites, were still carrying off the sheep, flying down upon them, and devouring them. The sheep were silent, but the dabela lamented and cried out.

(Enoch 89:17)
Then the ravens contended, and struggled with them.

(Enoch 89:18)
They wished among them to break his horn; but they prevailed not over him.

(Enoch 89:19)
I looked on them, until the shepherds, the eagles, the avest, and the kites came.

(Enoch 89:20)
Who cried out to the ravens to break the horn of the dabela; to contend with him; and to kill him. But he struggled with them, and cried out, that help might come to him.

(Enoch 89:21)
Then I perceived that the man came who had written down the names of the shepherds, and who ascended up before the Lord of the sheep.

(Enoch 89:22)
He brought assistance, and caused everyone to see him descending to the help of the dabela.

(Enoch 89:23)
I perceived likewise that the Lord of the sheep came to them in wrath, while all those who saw him fled away; all fell down in his tabernacle before his face; while all the eagles, the avest, ravens, and kites assembled, and brought with them all the sheep of the field.

(Enoch 89:24)
All came together, and strove to break the horn of the dabela.

(Enoch 89:25)
Then I saw, that the man, who wrote the book at the word of

the Lord, opened the book of destruction, of that destruction which the last twelve shepherds wrought; and pointed out before the Lord of the sheep, that they destroyed more than those who preceded them.

(Enoch 89:26)
I saw also that the Lord of the sheep came to them, and taking in his hand the scepter of his wrath seized the earth, which became rent asunder; while all the beasts and birds of heaven fell from the sheep, and sunk into the earth, which closed over them.

(Enoch 89:27)
I saw, too, that a large sword was given to the sheep, who went forth against all the beasts of the field to slay them.

(Enoch 89:28)
But all the beasts and birds of heaven fled away from before their face.

(Enoch 89:29)
And I saw a throne erected in a delectable land;

(Enoch 89:30)
Upon this sat the Lord of the sheep, who received all the sealed books;

(Enoch 89:31)
Which were open before him.

(Enoch 89:32)
Then the Lord called the first seven white ones, and commanded them to bring before him the first of the first

stars, which preceded the stars whose form partly resembled that of horses; the first star, which fell down first; and they brought them all before him.

(Enoch 89:33)
And he spoke to the man who wrote in his presence, who was one of the seven white ones, saying, Take those seventy shepherds, to whom I delivered up the sheep, and who receiving them killed more of them than I commanded. Behold, I saw them all bound, and all standing before him. First came on the trial of the stars, which, being judged, and found guilty, went to the place of punishment. They thrust them into a place, deep, and full of flaming fire, and full of pillars of fire. Then the seventy shepherds were judged, and being found guilty, were thrust into the flaming abyss.

(Enoch 89:34)
At that time likewise I perceived, that one abyss was thus opened in the midst of the earth, which was full of fire.

(Enoch 89:35)
And to this were brought the blind sheep; which being judged, and found guilty, were all thrust into that abyss of fire on the earth, and burnt.

(Enoch 89:36)
The abyss was on the right of that house.

(Enoch 89:37)
And I saw the sheep burning, and their bones consuming.

(Enoch 89:38)
I stood beholding him immerge that ancient house, while they brought out its pillars, every plant in it, and the ivory

infolding it. They brought it out, and deposited it in a place on the right side of the earth.

(Enoch 89:39)
I also saw, that the Lord of the sheep produced a new house, great, and loftier than the former, which he bounded by the former circular spot. All its pillars were new, and its ivory new, as well as more abundant than the former ancient ivory, which he had brought out.

(Enoch 89:40)
And while all the sheep which were left were in the midst of it, all the beasts of the earth, and all the birds of heaven, fell down and worshipped them, petitioning them, and obeying them in everything.

(Enoch 89:41)
Then those three, who were clothed in white, and who, holding me by my hand, had before caused me to ascend, while the hand of him who spoke held me; raised me up, and placed me in the midst of the sheep, before the judgment took place.

(Enoch 89:42)
The sheep were all white, with wool long and pure. Then all who had perished, and had been destroyed, every beast of the field, and every bird of heaven, assembled in that house: while the Lord of the sheep rejoiced with great joy, because all were good, and had come back again to his dwelling.

(Enoch 89:43)
And I saw that they laid down the sword which had been given to the sheep, and returned it to his house, sealing it up in the presence of the Lord.

(Enoch 89:44)
All the sheep would have been enclosed in that house, had it been capable of containing them; and the eyes of all were open, gazing on the good one; nor was there one among them who did not behold him.

(Enoch 89:45)
I likewise perceived that the house was large, wide, and extremely full. I saw, too, that a white cow was born, whose horns were great; and that all the beasts of the field, and all the birds of heaven, were alarmed at him, and entreated him at all times.

(Enoch 89:46)
Then I saw that the nature of all of them was changed, and that they became white cows;

(Enoch 89:47)
And that the first, who was in the midst of them, spoke, when that word became a large beast, upon the head of which were great and black horns;

(Enoch 89:48)
While the Lord of the sheep rejoiced over them, and over all the cows.

(Enoch 89:49)
I lay down in the midst of them: I awoke; and saw the whole. This is the vision which I saw, lying down and waking. Then I blessed the Lord of righteousness, and gave glory to him.

(Enoch 89:50)
Afterwards I wept abundantly, nor did my tears cease, so that I became incapable of enduring it. While I was looking on, they

flowed on account of what I saw; for all was come and gone by; every individual circumstance respecting the conduct of mankind was seen by me.

(Enoch 89:51)
In that night, I remembered my former dream; and therefore, wept and was troubled, because I had seen that vision.

~ ~ ~

(Enoch 90:1)
And now, my son Mathusala, call to me all your brethren, and assemble for me all the children of your mother; for a voice calls me, and the spirit is poured out upon me, that I may show you everything which shall happen to you forever.

(Enoch 90:2)
Then Mathusala went, called to him all his brethren, and assembled his kindred.

(Enoch 90:3)
And conversing with all his children in truth,

(Enoch 90:4)
Enoch said, Hear, my children, every word of your father, and listen in uprightness to the voice of my mouth; for I would gain your attention, while I address you. My beloved, be attached to integrity, and walk in it.

(Enoch 90:5)
Approach not integrity with a double heart; nor be associated

with double-minded men: but walk, my children, in righteousness, which will conduct you in good paths; and be truth your companion.

(Enoch 90:6)
For I know, that oppression will exist and prevail on earth; that on earth great punishment shall in the end take place; and that there shall be a consummation of all iniquity, which shall be cut off from its root, and every fabric raised by it shall pass away. Iniquity, however, shall again be renewed, and consummated on earth. Every act of crime, and every act of oppression and impiety, shall be a second time embraced.

(Enoch 90:7)
When therefore iniquity, sin, blasphemy, tyranny, and every evil work, shall increase, and when transgression, impiety, and uncleanness also shall increase, then upon them all shall great punishment be inflicted from heaven.

(Enoch 90:8)
The holy Lord shall go forth in wrath, and upon them all shall great punishment from heaven be inflicted.

(Enoch 90:9)
The holy Lord shall go forth in wrath, and with punishment, that he may execute judgment upon earth.

(Enoch 90:10)
In those days oppression shall be cut off from its roots, and iniquity with fraud shall be eradicated, perishing from under heaven.

(Enoch 90:11)
Every place of strength shall be surrendered with its

inhabitants; with fire shall it be burnt. They shall be brought from every part of the earth, and be cast into a judgment of fire. They shall perish in wrath, and by a judgment overpowering them forever.

(Enoch 90:12)
Righteousness shall be raised up from slumber; and wisdom shall be raised up, and conferred upon them.

(Enoch 90:13)
Then shall the roots of iniquity be cut off; sinners perish by the sword; and blasphemers be annihilated everywhere.

(Enoch 90:14)
Those who meditate oppression, and those who blaspheme, by the sword shall perish.

(Enoch 90:15)
And now, my children, I will describe and point out to you the path of righteousness and the path of oppression.

(Enoch 90:16)
I will again point them out to you, that you may know what is to come.

(Enoch 90:17)
Here now, my children, and walk in the path of righteousness, but shun that of oppression; for all who walk in the path of iniquity shall perish forever.

(Genesis 5:22) (...Jasher 3:1...)
And Enoch walked with God after he begot Methuselah three hundred years, and begot sons and daughters:

(Jasher 3:13...)
And these are the generations of Enoch, Methuselah, Elisha, and Elimelech, three sons; and their sisters were Melca and Nahmah.

(...Jasher 3:1)
And he served the Lord, and despised the evil ways of men.

(Jasher 3:2)
And the soul of Enoch was wrapped up in the instruction of the Lord, in knowledge and in understanding; and he wisely retired from the sons of men, and secreted himself from them for many days.

(Jubilees 4:21)
And he was moreover with the angels of God these six jubilees of years, and they showed him everything which is on earth and in the heavens, the rule of the sun, and he wrote down everything.

(Jubilees 4:22)
And he testified to the Watchers, who had sinned with the daughters of men; for these had begun to unite themselves, so as to be defiled, with the daughters of men, and Enoch testified against them all.

(Jasher 3:3)
And it was at the expiration of many years, while he was serving the Lord, and praying before him in his house, that an angel of the Lord called to him from Heaven, and he said, Here am I.

~ ~ ~

(Enoch 70: 1)
Afterwards my spirit was concealed, ascending into the heavens. I beheld the sons of the holy angels treading on flaming fire, whose garments and robes were white, and whose countenances were transparent as crystal.

(Enoch 70:2)
I saw two rivers of fire glittering like the hyacinth,

(Enoch 70:3)
Then I fell on my face before the Lord of spirits.

(Enoch 70:4)
And Michael, one of the archangels, took me by my right hand, raised me up, and brought me out to where was every secret of mercy and secret of righteousness.

(Enoch 70:5)
He showed me all the hidden things of the extremities of heaven, all the receptacles of the stars, and the splendors of all, from where they went forth before the face of the holy.

(Enoch 70:6)
And he concealed the spirit of Enoch in the heaven of heavens.

(Enoch 70:7)
There I beheld, in the midst of that light, a building raised with stones of ice;

(Enoch 70:8)
And in the midst of these stones vibrations of living fire. My spirit saw around the circle of this flaming habitation, on one of its extremities, that there were rivers full of living fire, which encompassed it.

(Enoch 70:9)
Then the Seraphim, the Cherubim, and Ophanin surrounded it these are those who never sleep, but watch the throne of his glory.

(Enoch 70:10)
And I beheld angels innumerable, thousands of thousands, and myriads of myriads, who surrounded that habitation.

(Enoch 70:11)
Michael, Raphael, Gabriel, Phanuel, and the holy angels who were in the heavens above, went in and out of it. Michael, Raphael, and Gabriel went out of that habitation, and holy angels innumerable.

(Enoch 70:12)
With them was the Ancient of Days, whose head was white as wool, and pure, and his robe was indescribable.

(Enoch 70:13)
Then I fell on my face, while all my flesh was dissolved, and my spirit became changed.

(Enoch 70:14)
I cried out with a loud voice, with a powerful spirit, blessing, glorifying, and exalting.

(Enoch 70:15)
And those blessings, which proceeded from my mouth, became acceptable in the presence of the Ancient of Days.

(Enoch 70:16)
The Ancient of Days came with Michael and Gabriel, Raphael and Phanuel, with thousands of thousands, and myriads of

myriads, which could not be numbered.

(Enoch 70:17)
Then that angel came to me, and with his voice saluted me, saying, You are the offspring of man, who is born for righteousness, and righteousness has rested on you.

(Enoch 70:18)
The righteousness of the Ancient of Days shall not forsake you.

(Enoch 70:19)
He said, On you, he shall confer peace in the name of the existing world; for from there has peace gone forth since the world was created.

(Enoch 70:20)
And thus, shall it happen to you forever and ever.

(Enoch 70:21)
All who shall exist, and who shall walk in your path of righteousness, shall not forsake you forever.

(Enoch 70:22)
With you shall be their habitations, with you their lot; nor from you shall they be separated forever and ever.

(Enoch 70:23)
And thus, shall length of days be with the offspring of man.

(Enoch 70:24)
Peace shall be to the righteous; and the path of integrity shall the righteous pursue, in the name of the Lord of spirits, forever and ever.

~ ~ ~

(Enoch 80:1)
He said, O Enoch, look on the book which heaven has gradually dropped down; and, reading that which is written in it, understand every part of it.

(Enoch 80:2)
Then I looked on all which was written, and understood all, reading the book and everything written in it, all the works of man;

(Enoch 80:3)
And of all the children of flesh on earth, during the generations of the world.

(Enoch 80:4)
Immediately after I blessed the Lord, the King of Glory, who has thus forever formed the whole workmanship of the world.

(Enoch 80:5)
And I glorified the Lord, on account of his long-suffering and blessing towards the children of the world.

(Enoch 80:6)
At that time, I said, Blessed is the man, who shall die righteous and good, against whom no catalogue of crime has been written, and with whom iniquity is not found.

(Enoch 80:7)
Then those three holy ones caused me to approach, and placed me on the earth, before the door of my house.

(Enoch 80:8)
And they said to me, Explain everything to Mathusala your son; and inform all your children, that no flesh shall be justified before the Lord; for he is their creator.

(Enoch 80:9)
During one year we will leave you with your children, until you shall again recover your strength, that you may instruct your family, write these things, and explain them to all your children. But in another year they shall take you from the midst of them, and your heart shall be strengthened; for the elect shall point out righteousness to the elect; the righteous with the righteous shall rejoice, congratulating each other; but sinners with sinners shall die,

(Enoch 80:10)
And the perverted with the perverted shall be drowned.

(Enoch 80:11)
Those likewise who act righteously shall die on account of the works of man, and shall be gathered together on account of the works of the wicked.

(Enoch 80:12)
In those days, they finished conversing with me.

(Enoch 80:13)
And I returned to my fellow men, blessing the Lord of worlds.

~ ~ ~

(Jasher 3:4)
And He said, Rise, go forth from your house and from the place where you hide yourself, and appear to the sons of men, in order that you may teach them the way in which they should go and the work which they must accomplish to enter in the ways of God.

(Jasher 3:5)
And Enoch rose up according to the word of the Lord, and went forth from his house, from his place and from the chamber in which he was concealed; and he went to the sons of men and taught them the ways of the Lord, and at that time assembled the sons of men and acquainted them with the instruction of the Lord.

(Jasher 3:6)
And he ordered it to be proclaimed in all places where the sons of men dwelt, saying, Where is the man who wishes to know the ways of the Lord and good works? Let him come to Enoch.

~ ~ ~

(Enoch 37:1)
The vision which he saw, the second vision of wisdom, which Enoch saw, the son of Jared, the son of Malaleel, the son of Canan, the son of Enos, the son of Seth, the son of Adam. This is the commencement of the word of wisdom, which I received to declare and tell to those who dwell upon earth. Hear from the beginning, and understand to the end, the holy things which I utter in the presence of the Lord of spirits. Those who were before us thought it good to speak;

(Enoch 37:2)
And let not us, who come after, obstruct the beginning of wisdom. Until the present period never has there been given before the Lord of spirits that which I have received, wisdom according to the capacity of my intellect, and according to the pleasure of the Lord of spirits; that which I have received from him, a portion of life eternal.

(Enoch 37:3)
And I obtained three parables, which I declared to the inhabitants of the world.

~ ~ ~

(Enoch 38:1)
Parable the first. When the congregation of the righteous shall be manifested; and sinners be judged for their crimes, and be troubled in the sight of the world;

(Enoch 38:2)
When righteousness shall be manifested in the presence of the righteous themselves, who will be elected for their good works duly weighed by the Lord of spirits; and when the light of the righteous and the elect, who dwell on earth, shall be manifested; where will the habitation of sinners be? And where the place of rest for those who have rejected the Lord of spirits? It would have been better for them, had they never been born.

(Enoch 38:3)
When, too, the secrets of the righteous shall be revealed, then shall sinners be judged; and impious men shall be afflicted in

the presence of the righteous and the elect.

(Enoch 38:4)
From that period those who possess the earth shall cease to be powerful and exalted. Neither shall they be capable of beholding the countenances of the holy; for the light of the countenances of the holy, the righteous, and the elect, has been seen by the Lord of spirits.

(Enoch 38:5)
Yet shall not the mighty kings of that period be destroyed; but be delivered into the hands of the righteous and the holy.

(Enoch 38:6)
Nor from there on out shall any obtain commiseration from the Lord of spirits, because their lives in this world will have been completed.

~ ~ ~

(Enoch 39:1)
In those days shall the elect and holy race descend from the upper heavens, and their seed shall then be with the sons of men. Enoch received books of indignation and wrath, and books of hurry and agitation.

(Enoch 39:2)
Never shall they obtain mercy, says the Lord of spirits.

(Enoch 39:3)
A cloud then snatched me up, and the wind raised me above

the surface of the earth, placing me at the extremity of the heavens.

(Enoch 39:4)
There I saw another vision; I saw the habitations and couches of the saints. There my eyes beheld their habitations with the angels, and their couches with the holy ones. They were entreating, supplicating, and praying for the sons of men; while righteousness like water flowed before them, and mercy like dew was scattered over the earth. And thus, it shall be with them forever and forever.

(Enoch 39:5)
At that time, my eyes beheld the dwelling of the elect, of truth, faith, and righteousness.

(Enoch 39:6)
Countless shall be the number of the holy and the elect, in the presence of God forever and forever.

(Enoch 39:7)
Their residence I beheld under the wings of the Lord of spirits. All the holy and the elect sung before him, in appearance like a blaze of fire; their mouths being full of blessings, and their lips glorifying the name of the Lord of spirits. And righteousness incessantly dwelt before him,

(Enoch 39:8)
There was I desirous of remaining, and my soul longed for that habitation. There was my antecedent inheritance; for thus had I prevailed before the Lord of spirits.

(Enoch 39:9)
At that time, I glorified and extolled the name of the Lord of

spirits with blessing and with praise; for he has established it with blessing and with praise, according to his own good pleasure.

(Enoch 39:10)
That place my eyes contemplated long. I blessed and said, Blessed be he, blessed from the beginning forever. In the beginning, before the world was created, and without end is his knowledge.

(Enoch 39:11)
What is this world? Of every existing generation those shall bless you who do not sleep in the dust, but stand before your glory, blessing, glorifying, exalting you, and saying, The holy, holy, Lord of spirits, fills the whole world of spirits.

(Enoch 39:12)
There my eyes beheld all who, without sleeping, stand before him and bless him, saying, Blessed be you, and blessed be the name of God forever and forever. Then my countenance became changed, until I was incapable of seeing.

~ ~ ~

(Enoch 40:1)
After this I beheld thousands of thousands, and myriads of myriads, and an infinite number of people, standing before the Lord of spirits.

(Enoch 40:2)
On the four wings, likewise of the Lord of spirits, on the four sides, I perceived others, besides those who were standing

before him. Their names, too, I know; because the angel, who proceeded with me, declared them to me, discovering to me every secret thing.

(Enoch 40:3)
Then I heard the voices of those upon the four sides magnifying the Lord of glory.

(Enoch 40:4)
The first voice blessed the Lord of spirits forever and forever.

(Enoch 40:5)
The second voice I heard blessing the Elect One, and the elect who suffer on account of the lords of spirits.

(Enoch 40:6)
The third voice I heard petitioning and praying for those who dwell upon earth, and supplicate the name of the Lord of spirits.

(Enoch 40:7)
The fourth voice I heard expelling the impious angels, and prohibiting them from entering into presence of the Lord of spirits, to prefer accusations against the inhabitants of the earth.

(Enoch 40:8)
After this I besought the angel of peace, who proceeded with me, to explain all that was concealed. I said to him, Who are those whom I have seen on the four sides, and whose words I have heard and written down? He replied, The first is the merciful, the patient, the holy Michael.

(Enoch 40:9)
The second is he who presides over every suffering and every affliction of the sons of men, the holy Raphael. The third, who presides over all that is powerful, is Gabriel. And the fourth, who presides over repentance, and the hope of those who will inherit eternal life, is Phanuel. These are the four angels of the Most High God, and their four voices, which at that time I heard.

~ ~ ~

(Enoch 45:1)
Parable the second, respecting these who deny the name of the habitation of the holy ones, and of the Lord of spirits.

(Enoch 45:2)
Heaven they shall not ascend, nor shall they come on the earth. This shall be the portion of sinners, who deny the name of the Lord of spirits, and who are thus reserved for the day of punishment and of affliction.

(Enoch 45:3)
In that day shall the Elect One sit upon a throne of glory; and shall choose their conditions and countless habitations (while their spirits within them shall be strengthened, when they behold my elect one), shall choose them for those who have fled for protection to my holy and glorious name.

(Enoch 45:4)
In that day, I will cause my elect one to dwell in the midst of them; will change the face of heaven; will bless it, and illuminate it forever.

(Enoch 45:5)
I will also change the face of the earth; will bless it; and cause those whom I have elected to dwell upon it. But those who have committed sin and iniquity shall not inhabit it, for I have marked their proceedings. My righteous ones will I satisfy with peace, placing them before me; but the condemnation of sinners shall draw near, that I may destroy them from the face of the earth.

~ ~ ~

(Enoch 46:1)
There I beheld the Ancient of Days, whose head was like white wool, and with him another, whose countenance resembled that of man. His countenance was full of grace, like that of one of the holy angels. Then I inquired of one of the angels, who went with me, and who showed me every secret thing, concerning this son of man; who he was; where he was; and why he accompanied the Ancient of Days.

(Enoch 46:2)
He answered and said to me, This is the Son of Man, to whom righteousness belongs; with whom righteousness has dwelt; and who will reveal all the treasures of that which is concealed: for the Lord of spirits has chosen him; and his portion has surpassed all before the Lord of spirits in everlasting uprightness.

(Enoch 46:3)
This son of man, whom behold, shall raise up kings and the mighty from their couches, and the powerful from their thrones; shall loosen the bridles of the powerful, and break in

pieces the teeth of sinners.

(Enoch 46:4)
He shall hurl kings from their thrones and their dominions; because they will not exalt and praise him, nor humble themselves before him, by whom their kingdoms were granted to them. The countenance likewise of the mighty shall he cast down, filling them with confusion. Darkness shall be their habitation, and worms shall be their bed; nor from that their bed shall they hope to be again raised, because they exalted not the name of the Lord of spirits.

(Enoch 46:5)
They shall condemn the stars of heaven, shall lift up their hands against the Most High, shall tread upon and inhabit the earth, exhibiting all their works of iniquity, even their works of iniquity. Their strength shall be in their riches, and their faith in the gods whom they have formed with their own hands. They shall deny the name of the Lord of spirits, and shall expel him from the temples, in which they assemble;

(Enoch 46:6)
And with him the faithful, who suffer in the name of the Lord of spirits.

~ ~ ~

(Enoch 47:1)
In that day the prayer of the holy and the righteous, and the blood of the righteous, shall ascend from the earth into the presence of the Lord of spirits.

(Enoch 47:2)
In that day shall the holy ones assemble, who dwell above the heavens, and with united voice petition, supplicate, praise, laud, and bless the name of the Lord of spirits, on account of the blood of the righteous which has been shed; that the prayer of the righteous may not be intermitted before the Lord of spirits; that for them he would execute judgment; and that his patience may not endure forever.

(Enoch 47:3)
At that time, I beheld the Ancient of Days, while he sat upon the throne of his glory, while the book of the living was opened in his presence, and while all the powers which were above the heavens stood around and before him.

(Enoch 47:4)
Then were the hearts of the saints full of joy, because the consummation of righteousness was arrived, the supplication of the saints heard, and the blood of the righteous appreciated by the Lord of spirits.

~ ~ ~

(Enoch 48a:1)
In that place, I beheld a fountain of righteousness, which never failed, encircled by many springs of wisdom. Of these all the thirsty drank, and were filled with wisdom, having their habitation with the righteous, the elect, and the holy.

(Enoch 48a:2)
In that hour was this son of man invoked before the Lord of spirits, and his name in the presence of the Ancient of Days.

(Enoch 48a:3)
Before the sun and the signs were created, before the stars of heaven were formed, his name was invoked in the presence of the Lord of spirits. A support shall he be for the righteous and the holy to lean upon, without falling; and he shall be the light of nations.

(Enoch 48a:4)
He shall be the hope of those whose hearts are troubled. All, who dwell on earth, shall fall down and worship before him; shall bless and glorify him, and sing praises to the name of the Lord of spirits.

(Enoch 48a:5)
Therefore, the elect and the concealed one existed in his presence, before the world was created, and forever.

(Enoch 48a:6)
In his presence he existed, and has revealed to the saints and to the righteous the wisdom of the Lord of spirits; for he has preserved the lot of the righteous, because they have hated and rejected this world of iniquity, and have detested all its works and ways, in the name of the Lord of spirits.

(Enoch 48a:7)
For in his name shall they be preserved; and his will shall be their life. In those days shall the kings of the earth and the mighty men, who have gained the world by their achievements, 1 become humble in countenance.

(Enoch 48a:8)
For in the day of their anxiety and trouble their souls shall not be saved; and they shall be in subjection to those whom I have chosen.

(Enoch 48a:9)
I will cast them like hay into the fire, and like lead into the water. Thus, they shall burn in the presence of the righteous, and sink in the presence of the holy; nor shall a tenth part of them be found.

(Enoch 48a:10)
But in the day of their trouble, the world shall obtain tranquility.

(Enoch 48a:11)
In his presence shall they fall, and not be raised up again; nor shall there be any one to take them out of his hands, and to lift them up: for they have denied the Lord of spirits, and his messiah. The name of the Lord of spirits shall be blessed.

~ ~ ~

(Enoch 48b:1)
Wisdom is poured forth like water, and glory fails not before him forever and ever; for potent is he in all the secrets of righteousness.

(Enoch 48b:2)
But iniquity passes away like a shadow, and possesses not a fixed station: for the Elect One stands before the Lord of spirits; and his glory is forever and ever; and his power from generation to generation.

(Enoch 48b:3)
With him dwells the spirit of intellectual wisdom, the spirit of

instruction and of power, and the spirit of those who sleep in righteousness; he shall judge secret things.

(Enoch 48b:4)
Nor shall any be able to utter a single word before him; for the Elect One is in the presence of the Lord of spirits, according to his own pleasure.

~ ~ ~

(Enoch 49:1)
In those days, the saints and the chosen shall undergo a change. The light of day shall rest upon them; and the splendor and glory of the saints shall be changed.

(Enoch 49:2)
In the day of trouble evil shall be heaped up upon sinners; but the righteous shall triumph in the name of the Lord of spirits.

(Enoch 49:3)
Others shall be made to see, that they must repent, and forsake the works of their hands; and that glory awaits them not in the presence of the Lord of spirits; yet that by his name they may be saved. The Lord of spirits will have compassion on them: for great is his mercy; and righteousness is in his judgment, and in the presence of his glory; nor in his judgment shall iniquity stand. He who repents not before him shall perish.

(Enoch 49:4)
From here on out, I will not have mercy on them, says the Lord of spirits.

~ ~ ~

(Enoch 50:1)
In those days shall the earth deliver up from her womb, and hell deliver up from hers, that which it has received; and destruction shall restore that which it owes.

(Enoch 50:2)
He shall select the righteous and holy from among them; for the day of their salvation has approached.

(Enoch 50:3)
And in those days, shall the Elect One sit upon his throne, while every secret of intellectual wisdom shall proceed from his mouth; for the Lord of spirits has gifted and glorified him.

(Enoch 50:4)
In those days, the mountains shall skip like rams, and the hills shall leap like young sheep satiated with milk; and all the righteous shall become angels in heaven.

(Enoch 50:5)
Their countenance shall be bright with joy; for in those days shall the Elect One be exalted. The earth shall rejoice; the righteous shall inhabit it, and the elect possess it.

~ ~ ~

(Enoch 51:1)
After that period, in the place where I had seen every secret sight, I was snatched up in a whirlwind, and carried off westwards.

(Enoch 51:2)
There my eyes beheld the secrets of heaven, and all which existed on earth; a mountain of iron, a mountain of copper, a mountain of silver, a mountain of gold, a mountain of fluid metal, and a mountain of lead.

(Enoch 51:3)
And I inquired of the angel who went with me, saying, What are these things, which in secret I behold?

(Enoch 51:4)
He said, All these things which you behold shall be for the dominion of the messiah, that he may command, and be powerful upon earth.

(Enoch 51:5)
And that angel of peace answered me, saying, Wait but a short time, and you shall understand, and every secret thing shall be revealed to you, which the Lord of spirits has decreed. Those mountains which you have seen, the mountain of iron, the mountain of copper, the mountain of silver, the mountain of gold, the mountain of fluid metal, and the mountain of lead, all these in the presence of the Elect One shall be like a honeycomb before the fire, and like water descending from above upon these mountains; and shall become debilitated before his feet.

(Enoch 51:6)
In those days men shall not be saved by gold and by silver.

(Enoch 51:7)
Nor shall they have it in their power to secure themselves, and to fly.

(Enoch 51:8)
There shall be neither iron for war, nor a coat of mail for the breast.

(Enoch 51:9)
Copper shall be useless; useless also that which neither rusts nor consumes away; and lead shall not be coveted.

(Enoch 51:10)
All these things shall be rejected, and perish from off the earth, when the Elect One shall appear in the presence of the Lord of spirits.

~ ~ ~

(Enoch 52:1)
There my eyes beheld a deep valley; and wide was its entrance.

(Enoch 52:2)
All who dwell on land, on the sea, and in islands, shall bring to it gifts, presents, and offerings; yet that deep valley shall not be full. Their hands shall commit iniquity. Whatsoever they produce by labor, the sinners shall devour with crime. But they shall perish front the face of the Lord of spirits, and from the face of his earth. They shall stand up, and shall not fail forever and ever.

(Enoch 52:3)
I beheld the angels of punishment, who were dwelling there, and preparing every instrument of Satan.

(Enoch 52:4)
Then I inquired of the angel of peace, who proceeded with me, for whom those instruments were preparing.

(Enoch 52:5)
He said, These they are preparing for the kings and powerful ones of the earth, that thus they may perish.

(Enoch 52:6)
After which the righteous and chosen house of his congregation shall appear, from there on out unchangeable, in the name of the Lord of spirits.

(Enoch 52:7)
Nor shall those mountains exist in his presence, as the earth and the hills, as the fountains of water exist. And the righteous shall be relieved from the vexation of sinners.

~ ~ ~

(Jasher 3:7)
And all the sons of men then assembled to him, for all who desired this thing went to Enoch, and Enoch reigned over the sons of men according to the word of the Lord, and they came and bowed to him and they heard his word.

(Jasher 3:8)
And the spirit of God was on Enoch, and he taught all his men the wisdom of God and his ways, and the sons of men served the Lord all the days of Enoch, and they came to hear his wisdom.

(Jasher 3:9)
And all the kings of the sons of men, both first and last, together with their princes and judges, came to Enoch when they heard of his wisdom, and they bowed down to him, and they also required of Enoch to reign over them, to which he consented.

(Jasher 3:10)
And they assembled in all, one hundred and thirty kings and princes, and they made Enoch king over them and they were all under his power and command.

(Jasher 3:11)
And Enoch taught them wisdom, knowledge, and the ways of the Lord; and he made peace among them, and peace was throughout the earth during the life of Enoch.

(Jasher 3:12)
And Enoch reigned over the sons of men two hundred and forty-three years, and he did justice and righteousness with all his people, and he led them in the ways of the Lord.

(Jasher 3:14)
And it was in the fifty-sixth year of the life of Lamech when Adam died; he was nine hundred and thirty years old at his death, and his two sons, with Enoch and Methuselah his son, buried him with great pomp, as at the burial of kings, in the cave which God had told him.

(Jasher 3:15)
And in that place all the sons of men made a great mourning and weeping on account of Adam; it has therefore become a custom among the sons of men to this day.

(Jasher 3:16)
And Adam died because he ate of the tree of knowledge; he and his children after him, as the Lord God had spoken.

(Jasher 3:17)
And it was in the year of Adam's death which was the two hundred and forty-third year of the reign of Enoch, in that time Enoch resolved to separate himself from the sons of men and to secret himself as at first in order to serve the Lord.

(Jasher 3:18)
And Enoch did so, but did not entirely secret himself from them, but kept away from the sons of men three days and then went to them for one day.

(Jasher 3:19)
And during the three days that he was in his chamber, he prayed to, and praised the Lord his God, and the day on which he went and appeared to his subjects he taught them the ways of the Lord, and all they asked him about the Lord he told them.

(Jasher 3:20)
And he did in this manner for many years, and he afterward concealed himself for six days, and appeared to his people one day in seven; and after that once in a month, and then once in a year, until all the kings, princes and sons of men sought for him, and desired again to see the face of Enoch, and to hear his word; but they could not, as all the sons of

men were greatly afraid of Enoch, and they feared to approach him on account of the Godlike awe that was seated on his countenance; therefore no man could look at him, fearing he might be punished and die.

(Jasher 3:21)
And all the kings and princes resolved to assemble the sons of men, and to come to Enoch, thinking that they might all speak to him at the time when he should come forth among them, and they did so.

(Jasher 3:22)
And the day came when Enoch went forth and they all assembled and came to him, and Enoch spoke to them the words of the Lord and he taught them wisdom and knowledge, and they bowed down before him and they said, May the king live! May the king live!

~ ~ ~

(Enoch 58:1)
In the five hundredth year, and in the seventh month, on the fourteenth day of the month, of the lifetime of Enoch, in that parable, I saw that the heaven of heavens shook; that it shook violently; and that the powers of the Most High, and the angels, thousands of thousands, and myriads of myriads, were agitated with great agitation. And when I looked, the Ancient of Days was sitting on the throne of his glory, while the angels and saints were standing around him. A great trembling came upon me, and terror seized me. My loins were bowed down and loosened; my reins were dissolved; and I fell upon my

face. The holy Michael, another holy angel, one of the holy ones, was sent, who raised me up.

(Enoch 58:2)
And when he raised me, my spirit returned; for I was incapable of enduring this vision of violence, its agitation, and the concussion of heaven.

(Enoch 58:3)
Then holy Michael said to me, Why are you disturbed at this vision?

(Enoch 58:4)
Before now has existed the day of mercy; and he has been merciful and long-suffering towards all who dwell upon the earth.

(Enoch 58:5)
But when the time shall come, then shall the power, the punishment, and the judgment take place, which the Lord of spirits has prepared for those who prostrate themselves to the judgment of righteousness, for those who abjure that judgment, and for those who take his name in vain.

(Enoch 58:6)
That day has been prepared for the elect as a day of covenant; and for sinners as a day of inquisition.

(Enoch 58:7)
In that day, two monsters shall be distributed for food; a female monster, whose name is Leviathan, dwelling in the depths of the sea, above the springs of waters;

(Enoch 58:8)
And a male monster, whose name is Behemoth; which possesses, moving on his breast, the invisible wilderness.

(Enoch 58:9)
His name was Dendayen in the east of the garden, where the elect and the righteous will dwell; where he received it from my ancestor, who was man, from Adam the first of men, whom the Lord of spirits made.

(Enoch 58:10)
Then I asked of another angel to show me the power of those monsters, how they became separated on the same day, one being in the depths of the sea, and one in the dry desert.

(Enoch 58:11)
And he said, You, son of man, are here desirous of understanding secret things.

(Enoch 58:12)
And the angel of peace, who was with me, said, These two monsters are by the power of God prepared to become food, that the punishment of God may not be in vain.

(Enoch 58:13)
Then shall children be slain with their mothers, and sons with their fathers.

(Enoch 58:14)
And when the punishment of the Lord of spirits shall continue, upon them shall it continue, that the punishment of the Lord of spirits may not take place in vain. After that, judgment shall exist with mercy and long-suffering.

~ ~ ~

(Enoch 60:1)
In those days, I beheld long ropes given to those angels; who took to their wings, and fled, advancing towards the north.

(Enoch 60:2)
And I inquired of the angel, saying, Why have they taken those long ropes, and gone forth? He said, They are gone forth to measure.

(Enoch 60:3)
The angel, who proceeded with me, said, These are the measures of the righteous; and cords shall the righteous bring, that they may trust in the name of the Lord of spirits forever and ever.

(Enoch 60:4)
The elect shall begin to dwell with the elect.

(Enoch 60:5)
And these are the measures which shall be given to faith, and which shall strengthen the words of righteousness.

(Enoch 60:6)
These measures shall reveal all the secrets in the depth of the earth.

(Enoch 60:7)
And it shall be, that those who have been destroyed in the desert, and who have been devoured by the fish of the sea, and by wild beasts, shall return, and trust in the day of the

Elect One; for none shall perish in the presence of the Lord of spirits, nor shall any be capable of perishing.

(Enoch 60:8)
Then they received the commandment, all who were in the heavens above; to whom a combined power, voice, and splendor, like fire, were given.

(Enoch 60:9)
And first, with their voice, they blessed him, they exalted him, they glorified him with wisdom, and ascribed to him wisdom with the word, and with the breath of life.

(Enoch 60:10)
Then the Lord of spirits seated upon the throne of his glory the Elect One;

(Enoch 60:11)
Who shall judge all the works of the holy, in heaven above, and he shall weigh their actions in a balance. And when he shall lift up his countenance to judge their secret ways in the word of the name of the Lord of spirits, and their progress in the path of the righteous judgment of God most high;

(Enoch 60:12)
They shall all speak with united voice; and bless, glorify, exalt, and praise, in the name of the Lord of spirits.

(Enoch 60:13)
He shall call to every power of the heavens, to all the holy above, and to the power of God. The Cherubim, the Seraphim, and the Ophanin, all the angels of power, and all the angels of the lords, namely, of the Elect One, and of the other power, who was upon earth over the water on that day,

(Enoch 60:14)
Shall raise their united voice; shall bless, glorify, praise, and exalt with the spirit of faith, with the spirit of wisdom and patience, with the spirit of mercy, with the spirit of judgment and peace, and with the spirit of benevolence; all shall say with united voice: Blessed is He; and the name of the Lord of spirits shall be blessed forever and forever; all, who sleep not, shall bless it in heaven above.

(Enoch 60:15)
All the holy in heaven shall bless it; all the elect who dwell in the garden of life; and every spirit of light, who is capable of blessing, glorifying, exalting, and praising your holy name; and every mortal man, more than the powers of heaven, shall glorify and bless your name forever and ever.

(Enoch 60:16)
For great is the mercy of the Lord of spirits; long-suffering is he; and all his works, all his power, great as are the things which he has done, has he revealed to the saints and to the elect, in the name of the Lord of spirits.

~ ~ ~

(Jasher 3:23)
And in some time after, when the kings and princes and the sons of men were speaking to Enoch, and Enoch was teaching them the ways of God, behold an angel of the Lord then called to Enoch from heaven, and wished to bring him up to heaven to make him reign there over the sons of God, as he had reigned over the sons of men on earth.

(Jasher 3:24)
When at that time Enoch heard this he went and assembled all the inhabitants of the earth, and taught them wisdom and knowledge and gave them divine instructions, and he said to them, I have been required to ascend into heaven, I therefore do not know the day of my going.

(Jasher 3:25)
And now therefore I will teach you wisdom and knowledge and will give you instruction before I leave you, how to act on earth whereby you may live; and he did so.

(Jasher 3:26)
And he taught them wisdom and knowledge, and gave them instruction, and he reproved them, and he placed before them statutes and judgments to do on earth, and he made peace among them, and he taught them everlasting life, and dwelt with them some time teaching them all these things.

~ ~ ~

(Enoch 61:1)
Thus, the Lord commanded the kings, the princes, the exalted, and those who dwell on earth, saying, Open your eyes, and lift up your horns, if you are capable of comprehending the Elect One.

(Enoch 61:2)
The Lord of spirits sat on the throne of his glory.

(Enoch 61:3)
And the spirit of righteousness was poured out over him.

(Enoch 61:4)
The word of his mouth shall destroy all the sinners and all the ungodly, who shall perish at his presence.

(Enoch 61:5)
In that day shall all the kings, the princes, the exalted, and those who possess the earth, stand up, behold, and perceive, that he is sitting on the throne of his glory; that before him the saints shall be judged in righteousness;

(Enoch 61:6)
And that nothing, which shall be spoken before him, shall be spoken in vain.

(Enoch 61:7)
Trouble shall come on them, as on a woman in travail, whose labor is severe, when her child comes to the mouth of the womb, and she finds it difficult to bring forth.

(Enoch 61:8)
One portion of them shall look on another. They shall be astonished, and shall humble their countenance;

(Enoch 61:9)
And trouble shall seize them, when they shall behold this Son of woman sitting on the throne of his glory.

(Enoch 61:10)
Then shall the kings, the princes, and all who possess the earth, glorify him who has dominion over all things, him who

was concealed; for from the beginning the Son of Man existed in secret, whom the Most High preserved in the presence of his power, and revealed to the elect.

(Enoch 61:11)
He shall sow the congregation of the saints, and of the elect; and all the elect shall stand before him in that day.

(Enoch 61:12)
All the kings, the princes, the exalted, and those who rule over the earth, shall fall down on their faces before him, and shall worship him.

(Enoch 61:13)
They shall fix their hopes on this son of man, shall pray to him, and petition him for mercy.

(Enoch 61:14)
Then shall the Lord of spirits hasten to expel them from his presence. Their faces shall be full of confusion, and their faces shall darkness cover. The angels shall take them to punishment, that vengeance may be inflicted on those who have oppressed his children and his elect. And they shall become an example to the saints and to his elect. Through them shall these be made joyful; for the anger of the Lord of spirits shall rest on them.

(Enoch 61:15)
Then the sword of the Lord of spirits shall be drunk with their blood; but the saints and elect shall be safe in that day; nor the face of the sinners and the ungodly shall they from there on out behold.

(Enoch 61:16)
The Lord of spirits shall remain over them:

(Enoch 61:17)
And with this son of man shall they dwell, eat, lie down, and rise up, forever and ever.

(Enoch 61:18)
The saints and the elect have arisen from the earth, have left off to depress their countenances, and have been clothed with the garment of life. That garment of life is with the Lord of spirits, in whose presence your garment shall not wax old, nor shall your glory diminish.

~ ~ ~

(Enoch 62:1)
In those days, the kings who possess the earth shall be punished by the angels of his wrath, wheresoever they shall be delivered up, that he may give rest for a short period; and that they may fall down and worship before the Lord of spirits, confessing their sins before him.

(Enoch 62:2)
They shall bless and glorify the Lord of spirits, saying, Blessed is the Lord of spirits, the Lord of kings, the Lord of princes, the Lord of the rich, the Lord of glory, and the Lord of wisdom.

(Enoch 62:3)
He shall enlighten every secret thing.

(Enoch 62:4)
Your power is from generation to generation; and your glory forever and ever.

(Enoch 62:5)
Deep are all your secrets, and numberless; and your righteousness cannot be computed.

(Enoch 62:6)
Now we know, that we should glorify and bless the Lord of kings, him who is king over all things.

(Enoch 62:7)
They shall also say, who has granted us rest to glorify, laud, bless, and confess in the presence of his glory?

(Enoch 62:8)
And now small is the rest we desire; but we do not find it; we reject, and do not possess it. Light has passed away from before us; and darkness has covered our thrones forever.

(Enoch 62:9)
For we have not confessed before him; we have not glorified the name of the Lord of kings; we have not glorified the Lord in all his works; but we have trusted in the scepter of our dominion and of our glory.

(Enoch 62:10)
In the day of our suffering and of our trouble he will not save us, neither shall we find rest. We confess that our Lord is faithful in all his works, in all his judgments, and in his righteousness.

(Enoch 62:11)
In his judgments, he pays no respect to persons; and we must depart from his presence, on account of our evil deeds.

(Enoch 62:12)
All our sins are truly without number.

(Enoch 62:13)
Then shall they say to themselves, our souls are satiated with the instruments of crime;

(Enoch 62:14)
But that prevents us not from descending to the flaming womb of hell.

(Enoch 62:15)
Afterwards, their countenances shall be filled with darkness and confusion before the Son of Man; from whose presence they shall be expelled, and before whom the sword shall remain to expel them.

(Enoch 62:16)
Thus, says the Lord of spirits, this is the decree and the judgment against the princes, the kings, the exalted, and those who possess the earth, in the presence of the Lord of spirits.

~ ~ ~

(Enoch 69:1)
After this the name of the Son of Man, living with the Lord of spirits, was exalted by the inhabitants of the earth.

(Enoch 69:2)
It was exalted in the chariots of the spirit; and the name went forth in the midst of them.

(Enoch 69:3)
From that time, I was not drawn in the midst of them; but he seated me between two spirits, between the north and the west, where the angels received their ropes, to measure out a place for the elect and the righteous.

(Enoch 69:4)
There I beheld the fathers of the first men, and the saints, who dwell in that place forever.

~ ~ ~

(Jasher 3:27)
And at that time the sons of men were with Enoch, and Enoch was speaking to them, and they lifted up their eyes and the likeness of a great horse descended from heaven, and the horse paced in the air;

(Jasher 3:28)
And they told Enoch what they had seen, and Enoch said to them, On my account does this horse descend on earth; the time is come when I must go from you and I shall no more be seen by you.

(Jasher 3:29)
And the horse descended at that time and stood before Enoch, and all the sons of men that were with Enoch saw him.

(Jasher 3:30)
And Enoch then again ordered a voice to be proclaimed, saying, Where is the man who delights to know the ways of the Lord his God, let him come this day to Enoch before he is taken from us.

(Jasher 3:31)
And all the sons of men assembled and came to Enoch that day; and all the kings of the earth with their princes and counselors remained with him that day; and Enoch then taught the sons of men wisdom and knowledge, and gave them divine instruction; and he bade them serve the Lord and walk in his ways all the days of their lives, and he continued to make peace among them.

~ ~ ~

(Enoch 92:1)
After this, Enoch began to speak from a book.

(Enoch 92:2)
And Enoch said, Concerning the children of righteousness, concerning the elect of the world, and concerning the plant of righteousness and integrity.

(Enoch 92:3)
Concerning these things will I speak, and these things will I explain to you, my children: I who am Enoch. In consequence of that which has been shown to me, from my heavenly vision and from the voice of the holy angels have I acquired knowledge; and from the tablet of heaven have I acquired understanding.

(Enoch 92:4)
Enoch then began to speak from a book, and said, I have been born the seventh in the first week, while judgment and righteousness wait with patience.

(Enoch 92:5)
But after me, in the second week, great wickedness shall arise, and fraud shall spring forth.

(Enoch 92:6)
In that week, the end of the first shall take place, in which mankind shall be safe.

(Enoch 92:7)
But when the first is completed, iniquity shall grow up; and he shall execute the decree upon sinners.

(Enoch 92:8)
Afterwards, in the third week, during its completion, a man of the plant of righteous judgment shall be selected; and after him the plant of righteousness shall come forever.

(Enoch 92:9)
Subsequently, in the fourth week, during its completion, the visions of the holy and the righteous shall be seen, the order of generation after generation shall take place, and a habitation shall be made for them. Then in the fifth week, during its completion, the house of glory and of dominion shall be erected forever.

(Enoch 92:10)
After that, in the sixth week, all those who are in it shall be darkened, the hearts of all of them shall be forgetful of wisdom, and in it shall a man ascend.

(Enoch 92:11)
And during its completion he shall burn the house of dominion with fire, and all the race of the elect root shall be dispersed.

(Enoch 92:12)
Afterwards, in the seventh week, a perverse generation shall arise; abundant shall be its deeds, and all its deeds perverse. During its completion, the righteous shall be selected from the everlasting plant of righteousness; and to them shall be given the sevenfold doctrine of his whole creation.

(Enoch 92:13)
Afterwards there shall be another week, the eighth of righteousness, to which shall be given a sword to execute judgment and justice upon all oppressors.

(Enoch 92:14)
Sinners shall be delivered up into the hands of the righteous, who during its completion shall acquire habitations by their righteousness; and the house of the great king shall be established for celebrations forever. After, this, in the ninth week, shall the judgment of righteousness be revealed to the whole world.

(Enoch 92:15)
Every work of the ungodly shall disappear from the whole earth; the world shall be marked for destruction; and all men shall be on the lookout for the path of integrity.

(Enoch 92:16)
And after this, on the seventh day of the tenth week, there shall be an everlasting judgment, which shall be executed upon the Watchers; and a spacious eternal heaven shall spring forth in the midst of the angels.

(Enoch 92:17)
The former heaven shall depart and pass away; a new heaven shall appear; and all the celestial powers shine with sevenfold splendor forever. Afterwards likewise shall there be many weeks, which shall externally exist in goodness and in righteousness.

(Enoch 92:18)
Neither shall sin be named there forever and forever.

(Enoch 92:19)
Who is there of all the children of men, capable of hearing the voice of the holy one without emotion?

(Enoch 92:20)
Who is there capable of thinking his thoughts? Who capable of contemplating all the workmanship of heaven? Who of comprehending the deeds of heaven?

(Enoch 92:21)
He may behold its animation, but not its spirit. He may be capable of conversing respecting it, but not of ascending to it. He may see all the boundaries of these things, and meditate upon them; but he can make nothing like them.

(Enoch 92:22)
Who of all men is able to understand the breadth and length of the earth?

(Enoch 92:23)
By whom have been seen the dimensions of all these things? Is it every man who is capable of comprehending the extent of heaven; what its elevation is, and by what it is supported?

(Enoch 92:24)
How many are the numbers of the stars; and where all the luminaries remain at rest?

~ ~ ~

(Enoch 93:1)
And now let me exhort you, my children, to love righteousness, and to walk in it; for the paths of righteousness are worthy of acceptation; but the paths of iniquity shall suddenly fail, and be diminished.

(Enoch 93:2)
To men of note in their generation the paths of oppression and death are revealed; but they keep far from them, and do not follow them.

(Enoch 93:3)
Now, too, let me exhort you who are righteous, not to walk in the paths of evil and oppression, nor in the paths of death. Approach them not, that you may not perish; but covet,

(Enoch 93:4)
And choose for yourselves righteousness, and a good life.

(Enoch 93:5)
Walk in the paths of peace, that you may live, and be found worthy. Retain my words in your inmost thoughts, and obliterate them not from your hearts; for I know that sinners counsel men to commit crime craftily. They are not found in every place, nor does every counsel possess a little of them.

(Enoch 93:6)
Woe to those who build up iniquity and oppression, and who lay the foundation of fraud; for suddenly shall they be subverted, and never obtain peace.

(Enoch 93:7)
Woe to those who build up their houses with crime; for from their very foundations shall their houses be demolished, and by the sword shall they themselves fall. Those, too, who acquire gold and silver, shall justly and suddenly perish. Woe to you who are rich, for in your riches have you trusted; but from your riches you shall be removed; because you have not remembered the Most High in the days of your prosperity: [you shall be removed, because you have not remembered the Most High in the days of your prosperity.

(Enoch 93:8)
You have committed blasphemy and iniquity; and are destined to the day of the effusion of blood, to the day of darkness, and to the day of the great judgment.

(Enoch 93:9)
This I declare and point out to you, that he who created you will destroy you.

(Enoch 93:10)
When you fall, he will not show you mercy; but your creator will rejoice in your destruction.

(Enoch 93:11)
Let those, then, who shall be righteous among you in those days, detest sinners, and the ungodly.

~ ~ ~

(Enoch 94:1)
O that my eyes were clouds of water, that I might weep over you, and pour forth my tears like rain, and rest from the sorrow of my heart!

(Enoch 94:2)
Who has permitted you to hate and to transgress? Judgment shall overtake you, you sinners.

(Enoch 94:3)
The righteous shall not fear the wicked; because God will again bring them into your power, that you may avenge yourselves of them according to your pleasure.

(Enoch 94:4)
Woe to you who shall be so bound by execrations, that you cannot be released from them; the remedy being far removed from you on account of your sins. Woe to you who recompense your neighbor with evil; for you shall be recompensed according to your works.

(Enoch 94:5)
Woe to you, you false witnesses, you who aggravate iniquity; for you shall suddenly perish.

(Enoch 94:6)
Woe to you, you sinners; for you reject the righteous; for you receive or reject at pleasure those who commit iniquity; and their yoke shall prevail over you.

~ ~ ~

(Enoch 95:1)
Wait in hope, you righteous; for suddenly shall sinners perish from before you, and you shall exercise dominion over them, according to your will.

(Enoch 95:2)
In the day of the sufferings of sinners your offspring shall be elevated, and lifted up like eagles. Your nest shall be more exalted than that of the avest; you shall ascend, and enter into the cavities of the earth, and into the clefts of the rocks forever, like conies, from the sight of the ungodly;

(Enoch 95:3)
Who shall groan over you, and weep like sirens.

(Enoch 95:4)
You shall not fear those who trouble you; for restoration shall be yours; a splendid light shall shine around you, and the voice of tranquility shall be heard from heaven. Woe to you, sinners; for your wealth makes you resemble saints, but your hearts reproach you, knowing that you are sinners. This word shall testify against you, for the remembrance of crime.

(Enoch 95:5)
Woe to you who feed upon the glory of the corn, and drink the strength of the deepest spring, and in the pride of your power tread down the humble.

(Enoch 95:6)
Woe to you who drink water at pleasure; for suddenly shall

you be recompensed, consumed, and withered, because you have forsaken the fountain of life.

(Enoch 95:7)
Woe to you who act iniquitously, fraudulently, and blasphemously; there shall be a remembrance against you for evil.

(Enoch 95:8)
Woe to you, you powerful, who with power strike down righteousness; for the day of your destruction shall come; while at that very time many and good days shall be the portion of the righteous, even at the period of your judgment.

~ ~ ~

(Enoch 96:1)
The righteous are confident that sinners will be disgraced, and perish in the day of iniquity.

(Enoch 96:2)
You shall yourselves be conscious of it; for the Most High will remember your destruction, and the angels shall rejoice over it. What will you do you sinners, and where will you fly in the day of judgment, when you shall hear the words of the prayer of the righteous?

(Enoch 96:3)
You are not like them who in this respect witness against you; you are associates of SINNERS.

(Enoch 96:4)
In those days shall the prayers of the righteous come up before the Lord. When the day of your judgment shall arrive; and every circumstance of your iniquity be related before the great and the holy one;

(Enoch 96:5)
Your faces shall be covered with shame; while every deed, strengthened by crime, shall be rejected.

(Enoch 96:6)
Woe to you, sinners, who in the midst of the sea, and on dry land, are those against whom an evil record exists. Woe to you who squander silver and gold, not obtained in righteousness, and say, we are rich, possess wealth, and have acquired everything which we can desire.

(Enoch 96:7)
Now then will we do whatsoever we are disposed to do; for we have amassed silver; our barns are full, and the husbandmen of our families are like overflowing water.

(Enoch 96:8)
Like water shall your falsehood pass away; for your wealth will not be permanent, but shall suddenly ascend from you, because you have obtained it all iniquitously; to extreme malediction shall you be delivered up.

(Enoch 96:9)
And now I swear to you, you crafty, as well as simple ones; that you, often contemplating the earth, you who are men, clothe yourselves more elegantly than married women, and both together more so than unmarried ones, everywhere arraying yourselves in majesty, in magnificence, in authority,

and in silver: but gold, purple, honor, and wealth, like water, flow away.

(Enoch 96:10)
Erudition therefore and wisdom are not theirs. Thus, they shall perish, together with their riches, with all their glory, and with their honors;

(Enoch 96:11)
While with disgrace, with slaughter, and in extreme penury, shall their spirits be thrust into a furnace of fire.

(Enoch 96:12)
I have sworn to you, you sinners, that neither mountain nor hill has been or shall be subservient to woman.

(Enoch 96:13)
Neither in this way has crime been sent down to us upon earth, but men of their own heads have invented it; and greatly shall those who give it efficiency be execrated.

(Enoch 96:14)
Barrenness shall not be previously inflicted on woman; but on account of the work of her hands shall she die childless.

(Enoch 96:15)
I have sworn to you, you sinners, by the holy and the great one, that all your evil deeds are disclosed in the heavens; and that none of your oppressive acts are concealed and secret.

(Enoch 96:16)
Think not in your minds, neither say in your hearts, that every crime is not manifested and seen. In heaven it is daily written down before the Most High. From here on out, it shall

be manifested; for every act of oppression which you commit shall be daily recorded, until the period of your condemnation.

(Enoch 96:17)
Woe to you, you simple ones, for you shall perish in your simplicity. To the wise you will not listen, and that which is good you shall not obtain.

(Enoch 96:18)
Now therefore know that you are destined to the day of destruction; nor hope that sinners shall live; but in process of time you shall die; for you are not marked for redemption;

(Enoch 96:19)
But are destined to the day of the great judgment, to the day of distress, and the extreme ignominy of your souls.

(Enoch 96:20)
Woe to you, you obdurate in heart, who commit crime, and feed on blood. Where is it that you feed on good things, drink, and are satiated? Is it not because our Lord, the Most High, has abundantly supplied every good thing upon earth? To you there shall not be peace.

(Enoch 96:21)
Woe to you who love the deeds of iniquity. Why do you hope for that which is good? Know that you shall be given up into the hands of the righteous; who shall cut off your necks, slay you, and show you no compassion.

(Enoch 96:22)
Woe to you who rejoice in the trouble of the righteous; for a grave shall not be dug for you.

(Enoch 96:23)
Woe to you who frustrate the word of the righteous; for to you there shall be no hope of life.

(Enoch 96:24)
Woe to you who write down the word of falsehood, and the word of the wicked; for their falsehood they record, that they may hear and not forget folly.

(Enoch 96:25)
To them there shall be no peace; but they shall surely die suddenly.

~ ~ ~

(Enoch 97:1)
Woe to them who act impiously, who laud and honor the word of falsehood. You have been lost in perdition; and have never led a virtuous life.

(Enoch 97:2)
Woe to you who change the words of integrity. They transgress against the everlasting decree;

(Enoch 97:3)
And cause the heads of those who are not sinners to be trodden down upon the earth.

(Enoch 97:4)
In those days you, O you righteous, shall have been deemed worthy of having your prayers rise up in remembrance; and

shall have deposited them in testimony before the angels, that they might record the sins of sinners in the presence of the Most High.

(Enoch 97:5)
In those days, the nations shall he overthrown; but the families of the nations shall rise again in the day of perdition.

(Enoch 97:6)
In those days, they who become pregnant shall go forth, carry off their children, and forsake them. Their offspring shall slip from them, and while suckling them shall they forsake them; they shall never return to them, and never instruct their beloved.

(Enoch 97:7)
Again, I swear to you, you sinners, that crime has been prepared for the day of blood, which never ceases.

(Enoch 97:8)
They shall worship stones, and engrave golden, silver, and wooden images. They shall worship impure spirits, demons, and every idol, in temples; but no help shall be obtained for them. Their hearts shall become impious through their folly, and their eyes be blinded with mental superstition. In their visionary dreams shall they be impious and superstitious, lying in all their actions, and worshipping a stone. Altogether shall they perish.

(Enoch 97:9)
But in those days blessed shall they be, to whom the word of wisdom is delivered; who point out and pursue the path of the Most High; who walk in the way of righteousness, and who act not impiously with the impious.

(Enoch 97:10)
They shall be saved.

(Enoch 97:11)
Woe to you who expand the crime of your neighbor, for in hell shall you be slain.

(Enoch 97:12)
Woe to you who lay the foundation of sin and deceit, and who are bitter on earth; for on it shall you be consumed.

(Enoch 97:13)
Woe to you who build your houses by the labor of others, every part of which is constructed with brick, and with the stone of crime; I tell you, that you shall not obtain peace.

(Enoch 97:14)
Woe to you who despise the extent of the everlasting inheritance of your fathers, while your souls follow after idols; for to you there shall be no tranquility.

(Enoch 97:15)
Woe to them who commit iniquity, and give aid to blasphemy, who slay their neighbor until the day of the great judgment; for your glory shall fall; malevolence shall he put into your hearts, and the spirit of his wrath shall stir you up, that every one of you may perish by the sword.

(Enoch 97:16)
Then shall all the righteous and the holy remember your crimes.

~ ~ ~

(Enoch 98:1)
In those days shall fathers be struck down with their children in the presence of each other; and brethren with their brethren shall fall dead: until a river shall flow from their blood.

(Enoch 98:2)
For a man shall not restrain his hand from his children, nor from his children's children; his mercy will be to kill them.

(Enoch 98:3)
Nor shall the sinner restrain his hand from his honored brother. From the dawn of day to the setting sun shall the slaughter continue. The horse shall wade up to his breast, and the chariot shall sink to its axle, in the blood of sinners.

~ ~ ~

(Enoch 99:1)
In those days, the angels shall descend into places of concealment, and gather together in one spot all who have assisted in crime.

(Enoch 99:2)
In that day shall the Most High rise up to execute the great judgment upon all sinners, and to commit the guardianship of all the righteous and holy to the holy angels, that they may protect them as the apple of an eye, until every evil and every crime be annihilated.

(Enoch 99:3)
Whether or not the righteous sleep securely, wise men shall then truly perceive.

(Enoch 99:4)
And the sons of the earth shall understand every word of that book, knowing that their riches cannot save them in the ruin of their crimes.

(Enoch 99:5)
Woe to you, you sinners, when you shall be afflicted on account of the righteous in the day of the great trouble; shall be burnt in the fire; and be recompensed according to your deeds.

(Enoch 99:6)
Woe to you, you perverted in heart, who are watchful to obtain an accurate knowledge of evil, and to discover terrors. No one shall assist you.

(Enoch 99:7)
Woe to you, you sinners; for with the words of your mouths, and with the work of your hands, have you acted impiously; in the flame of a blazing fire shall you be burnt.

(Enoch 99:8)
And now know you, that the angels shall inquire into your conduct in heaven; of the sun, the moon, and the stars, shall they inquire respecting your sins; for upon earth you exercise jurisdiction over the righteous.

(Enoch 99:9)
Every cloud shall bear witness against you, the snow, the dew, and the rain: for all of them shall be withheld from you, that they may not descend upon you, nor become subservient to your crimes.

(Enoch 99:10)
Now then bring gifts of salutation to the rain; that, not being

withholders, it may descend upon you; and to the dew, if it has received from you gold and silver. But when the frost, snow, cold, every snowy wind, and every suffering belonging to them, fall upon you, in those days you will be utterly incapable of standing before them.

~ ~ ~

(Jasher 3:32)
And it was after this that he rose up and rode on the horse; and he went forth and all the sons of men went after him, about eight hundred thousand men; and they went with him one day's journey.

(Jasher 3:33)
And the second day he said to them, Return home to your tents, why will you go? Perhaps you may die; and some of them went from him, and those that remained went with him six day's journey; and Enoch said to them every day, Return to your tents, lest you may die; but they were not willing to return, and they went with him.

(Jasher 3:34)
And on the sixth day some of the men remained and clung to him, and they said to him, We will go with you to the place where you go; as the Lord lives, only death shall separate us.

(Jasher 3:35)
And they urged so much to go with him, that he ceased speaking to them; and they went after him and would not return;

(Jasher 3:36)
And when the kings returned they caused a census to be taken, in order to know the number of remaining men that went with Enoch; and it was on the seventh day that Enoch ascended into heaven in a whirlwind, with horses and chariots of fire.

(Jubilees 4:23)
And he was taken from among the children of men, and the angels conducted him into the Garden of Eden in majesty and honor, and behold there he writes down the condemnation and judgment of the world, and all the wickedness of the children of men.

(Jubilees 4:24)
And on account of it, God brought the waters of the flood on all the land of Eden; for there he was set as a sign and that he should testify against all the children of men, that he should recount all the deeds of the generations until the day of condemnation.

(Jubilees 4:25)
And he burnt the incense of the sanctuary, sweet spices acceptable before the Lord on the Mount.

(Jubilees 4:26)
For the Lord has four places on the earth, the Garden of Eden, and the Mount of the East, and this mountain on which you are this day, Mount Sinai, and Mount Zion will be sanctified in the new creation for a sanctification of the earth; through it will the earth be sanctified from all guilt and its uncleanness through- out the generations of the world.

(Genesis 5:23) (Jasher 4:1)
And all the days of Enoch, that Enoch lived on earth were

three hundred sixty- five years:

~ ~ ~

(Enoch 100:1)
Attentively consider heaven, all you progeny of heaven, and all you works of the Most High; fear him, nor conduct yourselves criminally before him.

(Enoch 100:2)
If he shut up the windows of heaven, restraining the rain and dew, that it may not descend upon earth on your account, what will you do?

(Enoch 100:3)
And if he send his wrath upon you, and upon all your deeds, you are not they who can supplicate him; you who utter against his righteousness, language proud and powerful. To you there shall be no peace.

(Enoch 100:4)
Do you not see the commanders of ships, how their vessels are tossed about by the waves, torn to pieces by the winds, and exposed to the greatest peril?

(Enoch 100:5)
That they therefore fear, because their whole property is embarked with them on the ocean; and that they forebode evil in their hearts, because it may swallow them up, and they may perish in it?

(Enoch 100:6)
Is not the whole sea, all its waters, and all its commotion, the work of him, the Most High; of him who has sealed up all its exertions, and girded it on every side with sand?

(Enoch 100:7)
Is it not at his rebuke dried up, and alarmed; while all its fish with everything contained in it die? And will not you, you sinners, who are on earth, fear him? Is not he the maker of heaven and earth, and of all things which are in them?

(Enoch 100:8)
And who has given erudition and wisdom to all that move progressive upon the earth, and over the sea?

(Enoch 100:9)
Are not the commanders of ships terrified at the ocean? And shall not sinners be terrified at the Most High?

~ ~ ~

(Enoch 101:1)
In those days, when he shall cast the calamity of fire upon you, where will you fly, and where will you be safe?

(Enoch 101:2)
And when he sends forth his word against you, are you not spared, and terrified?

(Enoch 101:3)
All the luminaries are agitated with great fear; and all the

earth is spared, while it trembles, and suffers anxiety.

(Enoch 101:4)
All the angels fulfill the commands received by them, and are desirous of being concealed from the presence of the great glory; while the children of the earth are alarmed and troubled.

(Enoch 101:5)
But you, you sinners, are forever accursed; to you there shall be no peace.

(Enoch 101:6)
Fear not, you souls of the righteous; but wait with patient hope for the day of your death in righteousness. Grieve not, because your souls descend in great trouble, with groaning, lamentation, and sorrow, to the receptacle of the dead. In your lifetime your bodies have not received a recompense in proportion to your goodness, but in the period of your existence have sinners existed; in the period of execration and of punishment.

(Enoch 101:7)
And when you die, sinners say concerning you, "As we die, the righteous die. What profit have they in their works? Behold, like us, they expire in sorrow and in darkness. What advantage have they over us? From here on out are we equal. What will be within their grasp, and what before their eyes forever? For behold they are dead; and never will they again perceive the light." I say to you, you sinners, you have been satiated with meat and drink, with human plunder and rapine, with sin, with the acquisition of wealth and with the sight of good days. Have you not marked the righteous, how their end is in peace? For no oppression is found in them even to the day of their death. They perish, and are as if they were not, while

their souls descend in trouble to the receptacle of the dead.

~ ~ ~

(Enoch 102:1)
But now I swear to you, you righteous, by the greatness of his splendor and his glory; by his illustrious kingdom and by his majesty, to you I swear, that I comprehend this mystery; that I have read the tablet of heaven, have seen the writing of the holy ones, and have discovered what is written and impressed on it concerning you.

(Enoch 102:2)
I have seen that all goodness, joy, and glory has been prepared for you, and been written down for the spirits of them who die eminently righteous and good. To you it shall be given in return for your troubles; and your portion of happiness shall far exceed the portion of the living.

(Enoch 102:3)
The spirits of you who die in righteousness shall exist and rejoice. Their spirits shall exult; and their remembrance shall be before the face of the mighty one from generation to generation. Nor shall they now fear disgrace.

(Enoch 102:4)
Woe to you, sinners, when you die in your sins; and they, who are like you, say respecting you, blessed are these sinners. They have lived out their whole period; and now they die in happiness and in wealth. Distress and slaughter they knew not while alive; in honor they die; nor ever in their lifetime did judgment overtake them.

(Enoch 102:5)
But has it not been shown to them, that, when to the receptacle of the dead their souls shall be made to descend, their evil deeds shall become their greatest torment? Into darkness, into the snare, and into the flame, which shall burn to the great judgment, shall their spirits enter; and the great judgment shall take effect forever and forever.

(Enoch 102:6)
Woe to you; for to you there shall be no peace. Neither can you say to the righteous, and to the good who are alive, "in the days of our trouble have we been afflicted; every species of trouble have we seen, and many evil things have suffered.

(Enoch 102:7)
"Our spirits have been consumed, lessened, and diminished.

(Enoch 102:8)
"We have perished; nor has there been a possibility of help for us in word or in deed: we have found none, but have been tormented and destroyed.

(Enoch 102:9)
"We have not expected to live day after day.

(Enoch 102:10)
"We hoped indeed to have been the head;

(Enoch 102:12)
"But we have become the tail. We have been afflicted, when we have exerted ourselves; but we have been devoured by sinners and the ungodly; their yoke has been heavy upon us.

(Enoch 102:13)
"Those have exercised dominion over us who detest and who goad us; and to those who hate us have we humbled our neck; but they have shown no compassion towards us.

(Enoch 102:14)
"We have been desirous of escaping from them, that we might fly away and be at rest; but we have found no place to which we could fly, and be secure from them. We have sought an asylum with princes in our distress, and have cried out to those who were devouring us; but our cry has not been regarded, nor have they been disposed to hear our voice;

(Enoch 102:15)
"But rather to assist those who plunder and devour us; those who diminish us, and hide their oppression; who remove not their yoke from us, but devour, enervate, and slay us; who conceal our slaughter, nor remember that they have lifted up their hands against us."

~ ~ ~

(Enoch 103:1)
I swear to you, you righteous, that in heaven the angels record your goodness before the glory of the mighty one.

(Enoch 103:2)
Wait with patient hope; for formerly you have been disgraced with evil and with affliction; but now shall you shine like the luminaries of heaven. You shall be seen, and the gates of heaven shall be opened to you. Your cries have cried for

judgment; and it has appeared to you: for an account of all your sufferings shall be required from the princes, and from everyone who has assisted your plunderers.

(Enoch 103:3)
Wait with patient hope; nor relinquish your confidence; for great joy shall be yours, like that of the angels in heaven. Conduct yourselves as you may, still you shall not be concealed in the day of the great judgment. You shall not be found like sinners; and eternal condemnation shall be far from you, so long as the world exists.

(Enoch 103:4)
And now fear not, you righteous, when you see sinners flourishing and prosperous in their ways.

(Enoch 103:5)
Be not associates with them; but keep yourselves at a distance from their oppression; be you associated with the host of heaven. You, you sinners, say, All our transgressions shall not be taken account of, and be recorded. But all your transgressions shall be recorded daily.

(Enoch 103:6)
And be assured by me, that light and darkness, day and night, behold all your transgressions. Be not impious in your thoughts; lie not; surrender not the word of uprightness; lie not against the word of the holy and the mighty one; glorify not your idols; for all your lying and all your impiety is not for righteousness, but for great crime.

(Enoch 103:7)
Now will I point out a mystery: Many sinners shall turn and transgress against the word of uprightness.

(Enoch 103:8)
They shall speak evil things; they shall utter falsehood; execute great undertakings; and compose books in their own words. But when they shall write all my words correctly in their own languages,

(Enoch 103:9)
They shall neither change or diminish them; but shall write them all correctly; all which from the first I have uttered concerning them.

(Enoch 103:10)
Another mystery also I point out. To the righteous and the wise shall be given books of joy, of integrity, and of great wisdom. To them shall books be given, in which they shall believe;

(Enoch 103:11)
And in which they shall rejoice. And all the righteous shall be rewarded, who from these shall acquire the knowledge of every upright path.

~ ~ ~

(Enoch 104:1)
In those days, says the Lord, they shall call to the children of the earth, and make them listen to their wisdom. Show them that you are their leaders;

(Enoch 104:2)
And that remuneration shall take place over the whole earth; for I and my son will forever hold communion with them in

the paths of uprightness, while they are still alive. Peace shall be yours. Rejoice, children of integrity, in the truth.

~ ~ ~

(Genesis 5:24)

And Enoch walked with God: and he was not; for God took him.

(Jasher 3:37)
And on the eighth day all the kings that had been with Enoch sent to bring back the number of men that were with Enoch, in that place from which he ascended into heaven.

(Jasher 3:38)
And all those kings went to the place and they found the earth there filled with snow, and on the snow were large stones of snow, and one said to the other, Come, let us break through the snow and see, perhaps the men that remained with Enoch are dead, and are now under the stones of snow, and they searched but could not find him, for he had ascended into heaven.

(Jubilees 4:27...)
And in the fourteenth jubilee, Methuselah took to himself a wife, Edna the daughter of Azrial, the daughter of his father's brother, in the third week, in the first year of this week.

(Genesis 5:25) (...Jasher 3:13) (...Jubilees 4:27)

And Methuselah lived a hundred eighty-seven years, and begot a son and called his name Lamech:

(Jasher 4:2)
And when Enoch had ascended into heaven, all the kings of the earth rose and took Methuselah his son and anointed him, and they caused him to reign over them in the place of his father.

(Jasher 4:3)
And Methuselah acted uprightly in the sight of God, as his father Enoch had taught him, and he likewise during the whole of his life taught the sons of men wisdom, knowledge and the fear of God, and he did not turn from the good way either to the right or to the left.

(Jasher 4:4)
But in the latter days of Methuselah, the sons of men turned from the Lord, they corrupted the earth, they robbed and plundered each other, and they rebelled against God and they transgressed, and they corrupted their ways, and would not hearken to the voice of Methuselah, but rebelled against him.

(Jasher 4:5)
And the Lord was exceedingly wroth against them, and the Lord continued to destroy the seed in those days, so that there was neither sowing nor reaping in the earth.

(Jasher 4:6)
For when they sowed the ground in order that they might obtain food for their support, behold, thorns and thistles were produced which they did not sow.

(Jasher 4:7)
And still the sons of men did not turn from their evil ways, and their hands were still extended to do evil in the sight of God, and they provoked the Lord with their evil ways, and the

Lord was very wroth, and repented that he had made man.

(Jasher 4:8)
And he thought to destroy and annihilate them and he did so.

(Jasher 4:9)
In those days when Lamech the son of Methuselah was one hundred and sixty years old, Seth the son of Adam died.

(Genesis 5:26)
And Methuselah lived after he begot Lamech seven hundred eighty and two years, and begot sons and daughters:

(Genesis 5:27)
And all the days of Methuselah were nine hundred sixty and nine years: and he died.

(Jasher 4:11)
And Lamech was one hundred and eighty years old when he took Ashmua, the daughter of Elishaa the son of Enoch his uncle, and she conceived.

(Jasher 4:12)
And at that time the sons of men sowed the ground, and a little food was produced, yet the sons of men did not turn from their evil ways, and they trespassed and rebelled against God.

(Genesis 5:28) (Jubilees 4:28...) (Enoch 105:1)
And Lamech lived a hundred eighty-two years. And after a time, in the fifteenth jubilee in the third week, my son Mathusala took a wife for his son Lamech, and her name was Betenos the daughter of Barakiil, the daughter of his father's brother.

(...Genesis 5:28) (Jasher 4:13) (...Jubilees 4:28...) (Enoch 105:2)
And in this week, the wife of Lamech became pregnant by him at that time, at the revolution of the year and she brought forth a son: the flesh of which was as white as snow, and red as a rose; the hair of whose head was white like wool, and long; and whose eyes were beautiful. When he opened them, he illuminated all the house, like the sun; the whole house abounded with light.

(Enoch 105:3)
And when he was taken from the hand of the midwife, opening also his mouth, he spoke to the Lord of righteousness. Then Lamech his father was afraid of him; and flying away came to his own father Mathusala, and said, I have begotten a son, unlike to other children. He is not human; but, resembling the offspring of the angels of heaven, is of a different nature from ours, being altogether unlike to us.

(Enoch 105:4)
His eyes are bright as the rays of the sun; his countenance glorious, and he looks not as if he belonged to me, but to the angels.

(Enoch 105:5)
I am afraid, lest something miraculous should take place on earth in his days.

(Enoch 105:6)
And now, my father, let me entreat and request you to go to our progenitor Enoch, and to learn from him the truth; for his residence is with the angels.

(Enoch 105:7)
When Mathusala heard the words of his son, he came to me

at the extremities of the earth; for he had been informed that I was there: and he cried out.

(Enoch 105:8)
I heard his voice, and went to him saying, Behold, I am here, my son; since you are come to me.

(Enoch 105:9)
He answered and said, On account of a great event have I come to you; and on account of a sight difficult to be comprehended have I approached you.

(Enoch 105:10)
And now, my father, hear me; for to my son Lamech a child has been born, who resembles not him; and whose nature is not like the nature of man. His color is whiter than snow; he is redder than the rose; the hair of his head is whiter than white wool; his eyes are like the rays of the sun; and when he opened them he illuminated the whole house.

(Enoch 105:11)
When also he was taken from the hand of the midwife, he opened his mouth, and blessed the Lord of heaven.

(Enoch 105:12)
His father Lamech feared, and fled to me, believing not that the child belonged to him, but that he resembled the angels of heaven. And behold I am come to you, that you might point out to me the truth.

(Enoch 105:13)
Then I, Enoch, answered and said, The Lord will effect a new thing upon the earth. This have I explained, and seen in a vision. I have shown you that in the generations of Jared my

father, those who were from heaven disregarded the word of the Lord. Behold they committed crimes; laid aside their class, and intermingled with women. With them also they transgressed; married with them, and begot children.

(Enoch 105:14)
A great destruction therefore shall come upon all the earth; a deluge, a great destruction, shall take place in one year.

(Enoch 105:15)
This child which is born to you shall survive on the earth, and his three sons shall be saved with him. When all mankind who are on earth shall die, he shall be safe.

(Enoch 105:16)
And his posterity shall beget on the earth giants, not spiritual, but carnal. Upon the earth shall a great punishment be inflicted, and it shall be washed from all corruption. Now therefore inform your son Lamech, that he who is born is his child in truth; and he shall call his name Noah, for he shall be to you a survivor. He and his children shall be saved from the corruption which shall take place in the world; from all the sin and from all the iniquity which shall be consummated on earth in his days. Afterwards shall greater impiety take place than that which had been before consummated on the earth; for I am acquainted with holy mysteries, which the Lord himself has discovered and explained to me; and which I have read in the tablets of heaven.

(Enoch 105:17)
In them I saw it written, that generation after generation shall transgress, until a righteous race shall arise; until transgression and crime perish from off the earth; until all goodness come upon it.

(Enoch 105:18)
And now, my son, go tell your son Lamech,

(Enoch 105:19)
That the child which is born is his child in truth; and that there is no deception.

(Genesis 5:29) (Jasher 4:14) (...Jubilees 4:28) (Enoch 105:20)
When Mathusala heard the word of his father Enoch, who had shown hint every secret thing, he returned with understanding, and he called the name of that child Noah, saying, The earth was in his days at rest and free from corruption, and Lamech his father called his name Menachem, saying, This one shall comfort us concerning our work and miserable toil of our hands in the earth because of the ground which the Lord God has cursed. Because Noah was to console the earth on account of all its destruction.

(Jasher 4:15)
And the child grew up and was weaned, and he went in the ways of his father Methuselah, perfect and upright with God.

(Genesis 5:30)
And Lamech lived after he begot Noah five hundred ninety and five years, and begot sons and daughters:

(Genesis 5:31) (Jasher 5:20)
And all the days of Lamech were seven hundred seventy and seven years: and he died.

(Jubilees 4:33)
And in the twenty-fifth jubilee, Noah took to himself a wife, and her name was Emzârâ, the daughter of Râkêêl, the

daughter of his father's brother, in the first year in the fifth week: and in the third year thereof she bore him Shem, in the fifth year thereof, she bore him Ham, and in the first year in the sixth week, she bore him Japheth.

(Genesis 5:32)

And Noah was five hundred years old: and Noah begot Shem, Ham, and Japheth.

Epilogue

(Enoch 105:21)
Another book, which Enoch wrote for his son Mathusala, and for those who should come after him, and preserve their purity of conduct in the latter days. You, who have labored, shall wait in those days, until the evil doers be consumed, and the power of the guilty be annihilated. Wait, until sin pass away; for their names shall be blotted out of the holy books; their seed shall be destroyed, and their spirits slain. They shall cry out and lament in the invisible waste, and in the bottomless fire shall they burn. There I perceived, as it were, a cloud which could not be seen through; for from the depth of it I was unable to look upwards. I beheld also a flame of fire blazing brightly, and, as it were, glittering mountains whirled around, and agitated from side to side.

(Enoch 105:22)
Then I inquired of one of the holy angels who was with me, and said, What is this splendid object? For it is not heaven, but a flame of fire alone which blazes; and in it there is the clamor of exclamation, of woe, and of great suffering.

(Enoch 105:23)
He said, There, into that place which you behold, shall be thrust the spirits of sinners and blasphemers; of those who shall do evil, and who shall pervert all which God has spoken by the mouth of the prophets; all which they ought to do.

For respecting these things there shall be writings and impressions above in heaven, that the angels may read them and know what shall happen both to sinners and to the spirits of the humble; to those who have suffered in their bodies, but have been rewarded by God; who have been injuriously treated by wicked men; who have loved God; who have been attached neither to gold nor silver, nor to any good thing in the world, but have given their bodies to torment;

(Enoch 105:24)
To those who from the period of their birth have not been covetous of earthly riches; but have regarded themselves as a breath passing away.

(Enoch 105:25)
Such has been their conduct; and much has the Lord tried them; and their spirits have been found pure, that they might bless his name. All their blessings have I related in a book; and he has rewarded them; for they have been found to love heaven with an everlasting aspiration. God has said, While they have been trodden down by wicked men, they have heard from them revilings and blasphemies; and have been ignominiously treated, while they were blessing me. And now will I call the spirits of the good from the generation of light, and will change those who have been born in darkness; who have not in their bodies been recompensed with glory, as their faith may have merited.

(Enoch 105:26)
I will bring them into the splendid light of those who love my holy name: and I will place each of them on a throne of glory, of glory peculiarly his own, and they shall be at rest during unnumbered periods. Righteous is the judgment of God;

(Enoch 105:27)
For to the faithful shall he give faith in the habitations of uprightness. They shall see those, who having been born in

darkness to darkness shall be cast; while the righteous shall be at rest. Sinners shall cry out, beholding them, while they exist in splendor and proceed forwards to the days and periods prescribed to them.

Final Notes

We hope your journey is enriched and you are blessed through the production of the **Ancient Texts and the Bible** series!

Minister 2 Others would like to hear from you. If you have comments or questions concerning our materials, or if you find errors in our projects, misspellings, or formatting issues. We work hard to provide quality materials, however, sometimes things can squeak by unnoticed. Your feedback is truly appreciated.

We love producing helpful, innovative books and we are grateful for your support! If you have enjoyed this production, please consider writing a review and letting others know about our materials.

If you would like to be updated when we release new books and other materials, please sign up for our e-newsletter on our website.

Thanks!

Minister 2 Others

Minister2others.com

www.ingramcontent.com/pod-product-compliance
Lightning Source LLC
Chambersburg PA
CBHW071300190726
48292CB00007B/2626
9781947751187